Irving Press, N.Y.

View from the Terrace of Columbia University.

THE DEDICATION OF THE NEW BUILDINGS

OF THE

UNION THEOLOGICAL SEMINARY

IN THE CITY OF NEW YORK

NOVEMBER 27, 28 AND 29, 1910

BROADWAY AND ONE HUNDRED AND TWENTIETH STREET

NEW YORK

CONTENTS

I

HISTORICAL STATEMENT

HISTORICAL STATEMENT

The Union Theological Seminary in the City of New York was founded by a group of Christian ministers and laymen of the Presbyterian Church who believed that it was wise to plant a training school for ministers in a great city. They met first October 10, 1835, and, after three intermediate meetings, constituted a Board of Directors by the election of ten ministers and fourteen laymen, November 9 and 16, 1835. This Board of Directors held its first meeting January 18, 1836, when it chose its officers, appointed its committees, adopted the Preamble, and proceeded to further business. January 18, 1836, is therefore regarded as the official date of the founding of the Seminary.

The Seminary was opened for instruction on Monday, December 5, 1836. The Legislature of the State of New York passed the Act of Incorporation, March 27, 1839, and this was accepted by the Board of Directors, December 20, 1839.

The Founders of the Seminary were Presbyterians of the broader type represented in the New School branch of the Church, and had many affiliations with New England Congregationalism. They had in view a service of wider boundaries than those of the Presbyterian Church alone. The Seminary has been from the outset independent of any ecclesiastical control. The only approach to this was that on May 16, 1870, a few months after the Reunion of the Old and New School wings of the Presbyterian Church in the United States of America, it conceded to the General Assembly of that Church the right of veto on the election of its Professors, in the interests of harmony within the Church, and of similarity of standing for all its Theological Seminaries. This concession was withdrawn October 13, 1892. Now, as heretofore, Union Seminary is ecclesiastically independent, according to the plan of its Founders, and the provisions of its Charter.

For many years the Directors and Professors gave their assent to the Westminster Standards, the exact formula varying from time to time. Since 1905 this requirement has ceased, and a new form of declaration has been provided, which secures the Christian character of the institution in more comprehensive terms. At the present time the Board of Directors and the Faculty include representatives of the Presbyterian, Congregational, Protestant Episcopal, Baptist, and Methodist Episcopal Churches.

The principles underlying the foundation of the Seminary were expressed in the Preamble adopted at the beginning by the Founders. The Preamble reads as follows:

Preamble

That the design of the Founders of the Seminary may be fully known to all whom it may concern, and be sacredly regarded by the Directors, Professors and Students, it is judged proper to make the following preliminary statement:

A number of Christians, both clergymen and laymen, in the cities of New York and Brooklyn, deeply impressed with the claims of the world upon the Church of Christ to furnish a competent supply of well-educated and pious ministers of the Gospel; impressed also with the inadequacy of all existing means for this purpose; and believing that large cities furnish many peculiar facilities and advantages for conducting theological education; having, after several meetings for consultation and prayer, again convened on the 18th of January, A. D. 1836, unanimously adopted the following resolutions and declarations:

1. Resolved, in humble dependence on the grace of God, to attempt the establishment of a Theological Seminary in the City of New York.

2. This Institution (while it will receive others to the advantages it may furnish) is principally designed for such young men in the cities of New York and Brooklyn as are, or may be, desirous of pursuing a course of theological study, and whose circumstances render it inconvenient for them to go from home for this purpose.

3. It is the design of the Founders to furnish the means of a full and thorough education, in all the subjects taught in the best Theological Seminaries in the United States, and also to embrace therewith a thorough knowledge of the standards of faith and discipline of the Presbyterian Church.

4. Being fully persuaded that vital godliness well proved, a thorough education, and a wholesome practical training in works of benevolence and pastoral labors, are all essentially necessary to meet the wants and promote the best interests of

the kingdom of Christ, the Founders of this Seminary design that its Students, living and acting under pastoral influence, and performing the important duties of church members in the several churches to which they belong, or with which they worship, in prayer-meetings, in the instruction of Sabbath-schools and Bible-classes, and being conversant with all the social benevolent efforts in this important location, shall have the opportunity of adding to solid learning and true piety, enlightened experience.

5. By the foregoing advantages, the Founders hope and expect, with the blessing of God, to call forth from these two flourishing cities, and to enlist in the service of Christ and in the work of the ministry, genius, talent, enlightened piety and missionary zeal; and to qualify many for the labors and management of the various religious institutions, seminaries of learning, and enterprises of benevolence, which characterize the present times.

6. Finally, it is the design of the Founders to provide a Theological Seminary in the midst of the greatest and most growing community in America, around which all men of moderate views and feelings, who desire to live free from party strife, and to stand aloof from all extremes of doctrinal speculation, practical radicalism and ecclesiastical domination, may cordially and affectionately rally.

Requirements of the Charter

The Charter provides that "equal privileges of admission and instruction, with all the advantages of the Institution, shall be allowed to students of every denomination of Christians."

In fact instruction is given not only in the doctrine and polity of the Presbyterian Church, but also in those of other leading Protestant Churches. The student body at the present time is made up of members of twenty-two different Christian bodies. All of these are urged to retain their original connection, and to enter the ministry of their respective churches. The endeavor is made to provide them all with what they need for effective service to their own people.

The New Buildings

The first Seminary building was at No. 9 University Place, and was dedicated December 12, 1838. In later years a few subsidiary buildings were acquired in Winthrop Place (or

Greene Street), the next parallel street to the east, and at the corner of Winthrop Place and Clinton Place (Eighth Street).

In 1884 the Seminary moved to its second home on Lenox Hill, where its important group of buildings, with the main entrance at 1200 (afterward 700) Park Avenue, was dedicated December 9, 1884. The generous benefactions of ex-Governor Edwin D. Morgan, supplemented by large gifts from D. Willis James, Esq., Morris K. Jesup, LL.D., and others, made this move possible.

In 1908 the work of constructing the Seminary's third group of buildings began. The Corner Stone was laid on Tuesday, November 17, 1908. The buildings were opened for instruction on September 28, 1910, and the services of Dedication took place on Sunday, Monday and Tuesday, November 27, 28, and 29, 1910.

This second move received its impulse and its chief support from the princely contributions of Daniel Willis James, Esq., for forty years a Director, and Vice President of the Board since November 17, 1898, to which after his death Mrs. James made large additions. Generous contributions to the Building Fund were also made by other persons, including Mr. John Crosby Brown, the late President of the Board of Directors.

A brief description of the buildings follows:—

Their architecture is the English Perpendicular Gothic. They occupy the double block bounded by Broadway, Claremont Avenue, 120th and 122d Streets, and form a large rectangle, enclosing a Quadrangle approximately 300 feet long and 100 feet wide. A part of the west side, however, is for the present unoccupied by any building.

A tower at the corner of Broadway and 120th Street contains the main entrance hall, rising through three stories. Its ceiling is vaulted with fan tracery. A wide circular stairway leads to the upper floors of the Library as well as to the classrooms and Professors' studies and offices in the Administration Building. This corner tower is designed to rise ultimately to a height of over 200 feet and will then be a striking feature of the group.

The Library building occupies the Broadway side from the Entrance Tower to the Library Tower opposite 121st Street. On the first floor are two rooms devoted to the Biblical, Christian and Missionary Museum and to the exhibition of rare books. Several Seminar rooms occupy the second and fourth floors. On the third floor is the Reference Library, 100 feet long by 40 feet wide, with an oak beamed ceiling. The rooms for library administration adjoin this. The library stack is beneath the Reference Library, and contains five levels which connect with various floors. The Library Tower rises over a vaulted drive-way with ornamental iron gates, the principal entrance to the Quadrangle.

The Broadway Tower opens also into the Administration Building, which extends along 120th Street. The offices of the Seminary are on the first floor; on the second and third floors are class-rooms and a large lecture room; the fourth and fifth are divided into offices and studies for Professors and Instructors. Both the Library and the Administration Building have access to a terrace, which rises above the main level of the Quadrangle at the south, and, from within, gives these buildings, with the Chapel, a fitting prominence.

The Chapel stands on Claremont Avenue, across the Quadrangle from the Library, its lofty tower rising on the axis of the Quadrangle in line with the Library Tower. This Chapel has been erected as a Memorial to the late D. Willis James, Esq., who was a Director of the Seminary for many years, and its largest benefactor. The great chancel window was designed and made in England by a firm which during four generations has produced some of the best work in the typical English Antique glass.

The President's house occupies the corner of 120th Street and Claremont Avenue. Between it and the Chapel is a low Cloister enclosing various service-rooms connected with the Chapel. On the Quadrangle side an interior Cloister connects the entire group of buildings.

An Apartment House bounds the Quadrangle on 122d Street, and provides residences for ten Professors.

The Students' Dormitory extends from 121st to 122d Street on Broadway and contains about one hundred and fifty sets of rooms. Most of these comprise a study with bedroom adjoining; a few sets consist of a study and two bedrooms. Ample toilet accommodations are provided on each floor. In the Library Tower, with direct access from the Dormitory, is a Social Room for the use of the Students.

The buildings are of native stone taken from the site, the window tracery and finished trimmings being of Indiana limestone. A marked detail of the ornamentation is the series of academic seals and shields, carved in this limestone, on several faces of the Administration Building and Library.

The buildings are fireproof throughout, are heated by steam

and lighted by electricity, and are ventilated in the most approved manner. The main heating and lighting plant of the group is placed underneath the Dormitory at the lowest point of the site.

The Quadrangle is turfed and will be planted, so as to form an attractive and quiet enclosure.

The architects of the buildings are Messrs. Allen & Collens of Boston, Mass.

II

THE EXERCISES OF DEDICATION

1 The Sunday Morning Service
2 The Communion on Sunday Afternoon
3 The Student Meeting on Monday Evening
4 The Alumni Meeting on Tuesday Morning
5 The Dedication Service on Tuesday Afternoon
6 The Dinner on Tuesday Evening.

THE EXERCISES OF DEDICATION

The Dedication services began on Sunday morning, November 27, at eleven o'clock, when a large congregation assembled in the Chapel, and the Dedication sermon was preached by the Reverend Professor Henry Sloane Coffin, D.D. In the afternoon the Communion was celebrated at four o'clock, the Reverend Anson P. Atterbury, D.D., and the Reverend Professor Arthur Cushman McGiffert, D.D., officiating.

On Monday evening at eight o'clock a meeting was held in the Chapel, designed specially for the students of the Seminary and their friends, at which addresses were delivered by the Reverend Professor William Adams Brown, Ph.D., D.D., and President Jacob Gould Schurman, Sc.D., LL.D.

On Tuesday morning at ten-thirty o'clock the Alumni gathered in the Chapel for the anniversary meeting of the Alumni Association. After an address of welcome by the President of the Association, the Reverend Henry W. Ballantine, D.D., addresses were delivered by the President of the Seminary, the Reverend Francis Brown, D.D., LL.D., and by representative alumni—the Reverend Henry Hamlin Stebbins, D.D., the Reverend William Pierson Merrill, D.D., and the Reverend Howard Sweetser Bliss, D.D. At the conclusion of the service the alumni and invited guests adjourned to the large Lecture Room A, where luncheon had been provided by the Board of Directors.

The formal service of Dedication took place at three o'clock in the Chapel, admission being by ticket. The Presentation Address was made by Robert Curtis Ogden, LL.D., the President of the Board of Directors, to which the Reverend Francis Brown, D.D., LL.D., responded in behalf of the Faculty. The Dedication Prayer was offered by the Reverend Charles H. Parkhurst, D.D., the senior member of the Board. The Dedication Address was then delivered by the Reverend Charles Augustus Briggs, D.D., D.Litt., the senior member of the Faculty.

In the evening the visiting delegates and many friends and

guests of the Seminary were entertained at dinner by the Board of Directors at the Waldorf Astoria.

During Monday and Tuesday the buildings were open for inspection, and were visited by many of the delegates and friends of the institution. A brief account of the different services follows:

1. The Sunday Morning Service

The procession, which consisted of the Choir, the Faculty and the officiating persons, formed in the cloister and entered the Chapel during the organ voluntary played by Mr. William P. Dunn. The service was opened by the recitation of the Lord's Prayer, led by President Brown, after which the choir and congregation united in singing Hymn 405, "Soon May The Last Glad Song Arise." Professor George Albert Coe, Ph.D., LL.D., then read the Scripture lesson, Hebrews xi: 1–10, 17–27, 39, 40; xii: 1–2, after which the choir sang Chant 218, "Benedic, Anima Mea." The congregation then joined with President Brown in the Apostles' Creed, after which prayer was offered by the Reverend Professor Thomas Cuming Hall, D.D.

The usual offering for the Kingdom of God was then received, after which the Choir sang the anthem, "Hymn of Thanksgiving." The Dedication sermon was preached by the Reverend Henry Sloane Coffin, D.D., from the text, "Thou hast given me the heritage of those that fear thy name" (Psalm lxi: 5). President Brown then recited the collect for All Saints' Day, followed by the benediction: "O Almighty God, who hast knit together thine elect in one communion and fellowship, in the mystical body of thy Son Christ our Lord; grant us grace so to follow thy blessed Saints in all virtuous and godly living, that we may come to those unspeakable joys which thou hast prepared for those who unfeignedly love thee; through Jesus Christ our Lord.

"The peace of God, which passeth all understanding, keep your hearts and minds in the knowledge and love of God, and of his Son Jesus Christ our Lord; and the blessing of God Almighty, the Father, the Son, and the Holy Ghost, be amongst you and remain with you alway. AMEN."

The procession retired during an organ postlude by Mr. Dunn.

2. The Communion Service on Sunday Afternoon

The Choir and the officiating persons entered the Chapel during the organ prelude by Dr. Gerrit Smith. After the Lord's Prayer, in which the congregation were led by President Brown, the Choir sang Chant 15, "Venite." President Brown then read the Scripture lesson, John vi: 22-51, and the congregation joined in singing Hymn 599, "Lead us, O Father, in the paths of peace." The sacrament of the Lord's Supper was then observed, Professor McGiffert conducting the administration of the bread and the Reverend Anson P. Atterbury, D.D., the administration of the cup. After the singing by the congregation of Hymn 564, "Jesus my Lord, my God, my All," President Brown offered the concluding prayer, and pronounced the benediction as follows: "Grant, we beseech thee, O merciful Lord, to thy faithful people pardon and peace, that they may be cleansed from all their sins and serve thee with a quiet mind, through Jesus Christ our Lord.

"The grace of our Lord Jesus Christ and the love of God and the communion of the Holy Spirit, be with us all, evermore. AMEN."

The service closed with an organ postlude by Dr. Gerrit Smith.

3. The Student Meeting on Monday Evening

On Monday evening, November 28, at 8 o'clock, the procession, which consisted of the Choir, the Faculty and the officiating persons, entered the Chapel during an organ prelude by Dr. Gerrit Smith.

President Brown then led the audience in the Lord's Prayer, after which the Choir sang Chant No. 22, "Venite."

The Scripture Lesson, being Psalm cv, was read by the Reverend Professor George William Knox, D.D., LL.D., after which the Choir sang the anthem, "Hymn of Thanksgiving," Netherlands Hymn.

The Reverend Professor William Adams Brown, D.D., then delivered the Historical Address, at the conclusion of which the Choir, joined by the audience, sang Hymn No. 100, "All People That On Earth Do Dwell."

President Brown then introduced President Jacob Gould Schurman, Sc.D., LL.D., of Cornell University, in the following words:

"The next speaker comes to us from a busy life to say a word which he has deeply at heart. The subject of his address is to be 'Some Elements of Religious Progress.' I have great pleasure in presenting to a Union Seminary audience, President Jacob Gould Schurman, of Cornell University."

At the conclusion of President Schurman's address the Choir and audience joined in singing Hymn No. 352, "Lead On, O King Eternal." After this President Brown offered prayer and pronounced the benediction as follows:

"Almighty God, Father of all mercies, we, thine unworthy servants, do give thee most humble and hearty thanks for all thy goodness and loving kindness to us and to all men. We bless thee for our creation, preservation, and all the blessings of this life, and now in particular for thy goodness to this Seminary year after year, and for all its benefactors, supporters, teachers and friends; but above all for Thine inestimable love in the redemption of the world by our Lord Jesus Christ, for the means of grace and for the hope of glory, and, we beseech thee, give us that due sense of all Thy mercies that our hearts may be unfeignedly thankful, and that we may show forth thy praise not only with our lips but in our lives, by giving up ourselves to thy service and by walking before thee in holiness and righteousness all our days, through Jesus Christ, our Lord, to whom, with thee and the Holy Ghost, be all honour and glory, world without end. AMEN.

"The grace of our Lord Jesus Christ, the love of God and the fellowship of the Holy Spirit be with us all, evermore. AMEN."

The procession retired during an organ postlude by Dr. Gerrit Smith.

4. The Alumni Meeting on Tuesday Morning

The Alumni of the Seminary gathered in the Chapel on Tuesday morning, November 29, at half past ten o'clock, the Reverend Henry W. Ballantine, D.D., President of the Society of the Associated Alumni, presiding. The meeting was opened by an organ prelude, after which Dr. Ballantine offered the following Invocation:

"O God, our Heavenly Father, whose kingdom is everlasting, look graciously, we entreat thee, upon this gathering of thy servants, trained for the ministry of thy holy Gospel in this same Christian Seminary; but now for the first time finding ourselves in these spacious halls, which thou hast newly provided for us. We are filled with wonder and joy and hope, and yet we fear also.

" Unto thee, therefore, we look, the Protector of all who trust, without whom nothing is strong, nothing is holy. Increase and multiply upon us thy mercy, that, thou being our Ruler and Guide, we may so do our parts, both here in this place at this time and always hereafter in our sacred ministry, as to promote more and more effectually thy righteous kingdom, and so pass through things temporal that we finally lose not the things eternal.

" Grant this, O Heavenly Father, for the sake of Jesus Christ, our Lord. AMEN."

The Choir and audience then joined in singing Hymn No. 304, " The Church's One Foundation."

The Scripture Lesson, Psalm No. cxxii, was read by the Reverend Charles Ripley Gillett, D.D., the Secretary of the Associated Alumni.

The Reverend Joseph Dunn Burrell, D.D., then offered the following prayer:

" O God, our Heavenly Father, on this auspicious day we raise our hearts to Thee in thanksgiving and praise and as those who are the children of this institution especially we are grateful to Thee for what we see and know, and we bless Thee for what Thou didst for us through this Alma Mater, that Thou didst give us here that equipment which has enabled us to do something for Thee in the world, in the ministry of the Gospel of Jesus Christ. We are humbly grateful to Thee for that.

" And we look back over the years that are gone and think of the great number of those who went out from this school of learning, went out into the world and bore its burdens and did its work, and gave their hearts and lives to Thee, and have entered into eternal rest. We rejoice in that noble record. We pray that Thou wilt help us in our day and generation to be worthy of it.

"And we rejoice as we lift up our eyes and look into the future and see the great number who shall go out from these walls in the spirit of consecration to Thee to work in the world, and to make the world better by their presence in it, in the Spirit of Jesus Christ.

" O God, for all these things our hearts are grateful to Thee.

" Bless us now while we are here, this hour. Bless those who shall speak to us. May we gain something afresh of the spirit of this sacred place. May we gain anew the consecration of Jesus Christ our Saviour, and of Thee our loving God and Father. May we go away with our hearts burning within us with gratitude and love.

" These things we ask through Jesus Christ, our Lord. AMEN."

The Address of Welcome was given by the Rev. Dr. Ballantine, who spoke as follows:

" FELLOW ALUMNI:

" As I happen to be, by your favor, your presiding officer for the current year, there has come to me, among other pleasant incidents, to be chosen by the Directors and Faculty of the Seminary, to convey to you in their name a welcome to these new halls of study. In spaciousness and all manner of equipment they greatly surpass any we have hitherto known our loved Seminary to possess. They probably surpass the expectations of us all, either singly or together. It is probable they surpass the fondest dreams of most of us, even for our Seminary's distant future.

" Witnessing, as we have in recent years, the steady and even rapid enlargement and enrichment of the Seminary, some of the older graduates of us become almost bewildered. It is not our achievement. We of the Alumni have rarely been situated so as to lend even appreciable help. Under God these great enlargements are the work of the Directors and the Faculty, who have both devised and accomplished them.

" Let us not fail, therefore, on this day of dedication and henceforth, to give to them, the Directors and the Faculty, our hearty appreciation and their worthy meed of honor. And let us also thankfully embrace the opportunities afforded us from time to time to come in here and witness the Lord's work by these his servants.

" All our hearts are full to-day. Every one of us doubtless would like to give expression to some at least of the thoughts and feelings now welling up in our souls. But the limit of time forbids, all the time that is available being required for those who have been especially invited to address us.

" We will first hear a brief statement regarding the Cuthbert Hall Memorial Library Fund, from Professor William Adams Brown, to whom I now give way."

Professor Brown then made the following statement:

"MR. PRESIDENT AND FELLOW ALUMNI:

"It is with great pleasure that I stand here to make report on behalf of your Library Endowment Fund Committee, the stewardship of which you have entrusted to our care.

"Two separate tasks were committed to us: First, the raising of a general library fund, the income of which should be used for the purchase of books, and secondly, and more in particular, a special memorial fund to bear the name of our beloved President, Charles Cuthbert Hall, the income of which was to be used for the purchase of books on Christian Missions.

"I have before me the latest statement of the treasurer of the fund. He tells me that the general endowment fund consists up to date of $9,423.53, to which should be added in pledges $1,205.

"The Charles Cuthbert Hall Memorial Fund, I am glad to be able to announce to-day, is complete. This gratifying announcement is made possible through the generosity of an individual, himself a large donor to the fund, who had offered to guarantee the three hundred and odd dollars which are still lacking of the five thousand which we planned to raise.

"You will not misunderstand me, I am sure, if I say that those Alumni in whose heart it may lie to have some part in the completion of this work of love, have still a chance to assume to themselves any part of that remaining guarantee which they may desire, by communicating with Professor Rockwell, the Librarian, or with Dr. George S. Webster, the Secretary of the Fund.

"It may be interesting to know some of the facts connected with this Memorial Fund, which has been contributed by one hundred and fifty to two hundred donors, who have sent in amounts ranging from five hundred dollars to twenty-five cents. Any amount, however small, which you may desire to give in loving remembrance of Dr. Hall will be gratefully received by the Committee.

"If, to the contributions to the general fund, we add the pledges outstanding, the Charles Cuthbert Hall Memorial Fund, and one further generous gift by Mrs. R. Hall McCormick, secured through one of our Alumni, of five thousand dollars for the Henry Day Memorial Fund for the further care and completion of the Bird Hymnological Library, which was Mr. Day's gift, it will appear that the net result of the effort made two years ago, has been to increase the funds of our Library by over twenty thousand dollars, and I am sure you will hear this with gratification."

Dr. Ballantine then introduced the President of the Faculty, who delivered an address on "The Seminary's New Era."

At the conclusion of President Brown's address, Dr. Ballantine introduced the Reverend Henry Hamlin Stebbins, D.D., of the Class of 1867, who spoke on "The Claims of the Kingdom upon the Seminary."

Addresses followed by the Reverend William Pierson Merrill, D.D., of the Class of 1890, who spoke on "Our Gospel"; and the Reverend President Howard Sweetser Bliss, D.D., of the Syrian Protestant College at Beirût, whose subject was "The Christian Missionary and His Message in the Twentieth Century."

After the addresses were concluded, the Reverend Dr. Gillett, the Secretary of the Association, made the following announcements:

"I wish to call your attention to the announcement on the general program to the effect that there will be an informal luncheon at one o'clock to the Alumni and guests, which will be served in Room A, up one flight of stairs in the Administration Building.

"The interval until one o'clock is only about a quarter of an hour, but I think that we shall perhaps best spend it by remaining here in this room, rather than by making a very partial inspection of the buildings, though those who desire so to do have that opportunity.

"I hold in my hands four pamphlets, samples of those which have been placed in the vestibule on the table, and also in the entrance to the Memorial Tower. Those pamphlets consist of: (1) the Proceedings at the Laying of the Cornerstone and the Inauguration of Dr. Francis Brown as President of the Seminary, (2) an Address by the Reverend Charles Cuthbert Hall on 'Spiritual Expression and Theological Science,' (3) a pamphlet on the Seminary, its Spirit and Aims, containing addresses which were made on the occasion of the Annual Dinner of the Alumni Association held in 1907, and finally (4) a pamphlet by Dr. Charles Cuthbert Hall entitled, 'Notes of an Address before the Alumni of the Union Theological Seminary,' in the Adams Chapel, in 1903.

"At the conclusion of this service the Choir will pass out through the centre aisle and the rest of us, being all Alumni, will remain in this room, or proceed according to our own desire at one o'clock to the room where the luncheon will be served."

Professor William Adams Brown then made the following announcement:

"If our quarters were as large as our heart we could wish that every single alumnus could sleep in this building to-night. That is unfortunately impossible. There are, however, still a few single rooms in the building available for Alumni who may not be otherwise provided for, and as far as they go they are cordially at your service. If you will kindly communicate with Dr. McGiffert's office on the ground floor, he will see what can be done.

"The same is true of the dinner to-night. Here again we wish we could provide for everyone, but that I fear has not been possible, partly because we could not anticipate who would be here. I wish, therefore, to say that we have a number of tickets in the gallery which will be available for those alumni who will not attend the dinner, but who desire to hear the speeches which will be delivered. For these tickets also, will you kindly communicate with Dr. McGiffert or Professor Bewer. The seats in the gallery will be available at nine o'clock this evening and will afford an excellent opportunity to hear the speeches.

"Finally we wish everyone could be accommodated at the dedication services this afternoon, but because of the fact that a large number of delegates are coming from institutions all over the world, we shall have to deny ourselves the pleasure of including everyone of you, as we should wish, in the services this afternoon."

The Choir and audience then sang Hymn No. 358, "Who is On the Lord's Side?"

Prayer was then offered and the benediction pronounced by President Brown as follows:

"O Lord, who hast been our dwelling place in all generations we commit ourselves now to Thee, asking that Thou wilt guide us in the way that lieth before us, and that we may fear nothing so much as to lose touch with Thee; that if we see falsely Thou wilt enable us to see aright; that if we form wrong plans Thou wilt give us thy inspiration that we may change them to true plans; that in all things Thou wilt be with us, giving us Thy grace and enabling us more and more to learn of Thee through Jesus Christ.

"Help us, we beseech Thee, in the varied work of our lives. May each one in his daily round of service have Thy presence and the joy of it and Thy benediction and the success of it, and may we all together lift our hearts to Thee constantly in a union of praise for Thy goodness and love and serve Thee faithfully and obediently unto the end.

"We ask it for the sake of Jesus Christ our Lord. AMEN.

"The grace of our Lord Jesus Christ, the love of God and the fellowship of the Holy Spirit be with us all, evermore. AMEN."

The meeting closed with an organ postlude.

5. The Dedication Service

The formal service of Dedication was held in the Chapel of the Seminary at three o'clock on Tuesday afternoon, November 29.

The procession formed in the Administration Building, passed through the central door to the terrace which connects the Library and the Chapel, descended the steps to the interior court and, moving along the brick walk which bounds the quadrangle, entered the Chapel in the following order:

The Choir,
The Directors and Faculty of the Seminary,
The Representatives of other Institutions,
The Officiating Persons.

While the procession was forming, the Adagio from Guilmant's fifth sonata was played as an organ voluntary by Dr. Gerrit Smith, the Musical Director of the Seminary. The service opened with Hymn No. 139, "All Hail the Power of Jesus' Name," which was sung by the Choir as a processional.

The Reverend Francis Brown, D.D., President of the Faculty, then led in the recital of the Lord's Prayer, after which the Choir sang the anthem, "Except the Lord Build the House," by Gilchrist. The Reverend Joseph Dunn Burrell, D.D., then read the following Scripture lesson:

"Wherefore girding up the loins of your mind, be sober and set your hope perfectly on the grace that is to be brought unto you at the revelation of Jesus Christ; as children of obedience, not fashioning yourselves according to your former lusts in the time of your ignorance: but like as he who called you is holy, be ye yourselves also holy in all manner of living; because it is written, Ye shall be holy; for I am holy. And if ye call on him as Father, who without respect of persons judgeth according to each man's work, pass the time of your sojourning in fear, knowing that ye were redeemed, not with corruptible things, with silver or gold, from your vain manner of life handed down from your fathers; but with precious blood, as of a lamb without blemish and without spot, even the blood of Christ: who was foreknown indeed before the foundation of the world, but was manifested at the end of the times for your sake, who through him are believers in God, who raised him from the dead, and gave him glory; so that your faith and hope might be in God. Seeing ye have purified your souls in your obedience to the truth unto unfeigned love of the brethren, love one another from the heart fervently: having been begotten again, not of corruptible seed but of incorruptible, through the word of God, which liveth and abideth. For

"All flesh is as grass,
And all the glory thereof as the flower of grass,
The grass withereth and the flower falleth:
But the word of the Lord abideth forever.
And this is the word of good tidings which was preached unto you.

"Putting away therefore all wickedness, and all guile, and hypocrisies, and envies, and all evil speakings, as new-born babes long for the spiritual milk which is without guile, that ye may grow thereby unto salvation; if ye have tasted that the Lord is gracious: unto whom coming, a living stone, rejected indeed of men, but with God elect, precious, ye also, as living stones, are built up a spiritual house, to be a holy priesthood, to offer up spiritual sacrifices, acceptable to God through Jesus Christ. Because it is contained in the scripture, "Behold, I lay in Zion a chief corner-stone, elect, precious: And he that believeth on him shall not be put to shame."

(I. Peter i: 13; ii: 6.)

He added: "May God bless the reading of His Holy Word!"

The Choir then sang the Chant, No. 212, "Benedic Anima Mea."

The President of the Board of Directors, Robert Curtis Ogden, LL.D., made the address of Presentation, to which the President of the Faculty, the Reverend Francis Brown, D.D., made appropriate response.

The Dedicatory prayer was then offered by the Reverend Charles H. Parkhurst, D.D., the senior member of the Board, as follows:

" Thou divine Christ, Thou kindly Master, in whose presence we are gathered and under Whom we are seeking to serve, endue us with that appreciation of mind and spirit that shall qualify us to take the measure of this present occasion in all the variety of its sweet and solemn import, in its relation to the times past that have led up to this interesting but serious moment, in its relation to present obligation and opportunity, in its relation to the times forward to which we are looking and to which this institution is privileged and bound to bequeath in enlarged abundance its present possessions of strength, wisdom and grace.

" While confessing the earnestness with which our hearts are enlisted in this service of dedication, we are assured, O God, of Thine own divine interest in it, that Thy thought is engaged in it, that Thine eye, which is sensitive to whatever is fit and beautiful, rests with satisfaction upon that which has here been planned and constructed in Thy name, planned and constructed in attestation of our faith in Thee, in furtherance of Thy cause, in advancement of the interests of Thy kingdom.

" Thy guiding hand has been in all the history of this Seminary. In its bright days Thou hast gone before it as a pillar of cloud; in dark, difficult and troubled days, Thou hast led the way as a pillar of fire. In all our wanderings Thou hast kept us in Thy sight and we have ever striven to keep our faces toward Thee.

" Thou hast counselled this institution through the wisdom of men of large faith and of devout and loyal intention. Its foundations didst Thou lay in the intelligence and piety of men who could see with a long and wide vision and a pure heart, and as we revert to the years that are past, we bless Thee, dear Father, for the wealth of this Seminary's history and for all the power and impulse which survives as a sustaining and moving energy from those who have been the founders of that history and those who have been the shapers of its purposes and efforts.

" We gratefully remember this afternoon that from the first the prayerful aim has been to maintain here Christian doctrine that has been in simple line with Thine own revealed thought, doctrine that is faithful to that thought, both as narrow and as broad as that thought and as tender. We appreciate the heritage thus bequeathed to us, and now our prayer is that by Thy grace we, who are the heirs of the past, may be strong to stand erect and to walk unfalteringly under the blessed burden of that heritage.

" May Thy Spirit be the dominating influence in these halls, may this Seminary be spared the feebleness and the dishonour of becoming a scholastic institution, may the intelligence of those who teach and study here be of the clearest and finest, but intelligence held under the strictest control by a Christian devotement, with learning treated not as an end, but as a means, with a constantly cherished consciousness of its relation to the preaching of the Gospel of Jesus Christ: and these grounds, these buildings and all this splendid equipment made possible by the sanctified wisdom and genius of some who are living and of those who are gone, be cherished, all of it, as a holy temple dedicated to Thy service, O God, an instrument of Thy Church appointed for the salvation of the world.

" Continue to enrich with practical wisdom those who are charged with the responsibility of studying the material interests and administering the government of this institution. Endue with heavenly wisdom and prophetic vision those who are appointed to the service of instruction. May those who as students avail of the rich opportunities here offered enter these halls as disciples and emerge from them as young apostles full of divine light, power and purpose, men certified for the profound in their experience of the saving power of Christ and with all their hearts aglow with the Gospel message.

" And all this rich legacy of privilege and power into which as trustees and students we are now entered, all this superb dowry we do to-day with reverent and loving hearts dedicate to Thee, O God, Father, Son and Holy Spirit, praying Thee to hallow it all by Thy consecrating spirit that so it may be not only humanly fitted but *sanctified* to the work of publishing to the world the redemption wrought out by Jesus Christ our Lord. AMEN."

Dr. Ogden then introduced the senior Professor, the Reverend Charles Augustus Briggs, D.D., D.Litt., who delivered the Dedication Address, at the conclusion of which the Choir and Congregation sang Hymn No. 116, " Our God, Our Help in Ages Past." President Brown then offered prayer and pronounced the benediction as follows:

" Most glorious God; Accept through Thy beloved son Jesus Christ, our thanksgivings for Thine unspeakable love and goodness. Thou art the Father of mercies and God of all consolation, full of compassion, forgiving iniquity, transgression and sin. We thank Thee that thou hast founded Thy Church upon the Apostles and Prophets, Jesus Christ himself being the chief cornerstone. We thank Thee that Thou hast committed to Thy ministers the word of reconciliation. Continue Thy loving kindness unto us that we may rejoice and be glad in Thee all our days. Guide us by Thy counsel and afterward receive us to Thy glory; where with all the blessed host of heaven we may behold, adore, and perfectly and joyfully praise Thee, our most glorious Creator, Redeemer and Sanctifier, forever and ever, through Jesus Christ our Lord. AMEN.

"The peace of God, which passeth all understanding, keep your hearts and minds in the knowledge and love of God, and of his Son, Jesus Christ, our Lord, and the blessing of God Almighty, the Father, the Son and the Holy Ghost be amongst you and remain with you always. AMEN."

Then followed the Recessional, the Choir and Congregation singing Hymn No. 298, "Glorious Things of Thee are Spoken."

The services closed with an organ postlude, by Dr. Gerrit Smith, Lemmens' "Pontifical March."

6. The Dinner at the Waldorf-Astoria

The official delegates and a large number of the friends of the Seminary were entertained at dinner by the Board of Directors at the Waldorf-Astoria on Tuesday evening, November 29, at seven-thirty o'clock.

Tables were spread for five hundred and fifty guests, while the boxes in the gallery were occupied by many ladies and gentlemen, including a number of students of the Seminary.

The guests assembled in the large reception room on the Thirty-fourth Street side of the building and proceeded to the banqueting room, each of the guests at the speakers' table being escorted to his place by a member of the Board of Directors or of the Faculty.

The seating at the guests' table was as follows, beginning from the right:

*The Rev. Dean WILFORD L. ROBBINS, D.D., LL.D., General Theological Seminary.

*The Rev. EDWARD B. COE, D.D., LL.D., representing Robert College, Constantinople.

*The Rev. CHARLES H. PARKHURST, D.D., LL.D., Director of Union Theological Seminary.

* Unavoidably absent.

*The Rev. Amory H. Bradford, D.D., representing Mansfield College, Oxford, Eng.
The Rev. G. A. Johnston Ross, M.A., representing Westminster College, Cambridge, Eng.
The Rev. President James D. Moffat, D.D., LL.D., Washington and Jefferson College.
The Hon. John Wanamaker.
Jacob H. Schiff, Esq.
The Hon. St. Clair McKelway, LL.D., L.H.D., Vice-Chancellor, University of the State of New York.
Acting Chancellor John H. MacCracken, Ph.D., LL.D., New York University.
The Rev. President William H. P. Faunce, D.D., LL.D., Brown University.
The Rev. President James G. K. McClure, D.D., LL.D., McCormick Theological Seminary.
The Rev. Professor Edward C. Moore, Ph.D., D.D., Harvard University.
The Right Rev. David H. Greer, D.D., LL.D., representing Columbia University.
President Nicholas Murray Butler, Ph.D., LL.D., D.Litt., Columbia University.
President Robert C. Ogden, LL.D., L.H.D., Union Theological Seminary.
The Rev. President Francis Brown, Ph.D., D.D., LL.D., D.Litt., Union Theological Seminary.
The Rev. George Alexander, D.D., Moderator of the Presbytery of New York.
*The Rev. Professor Henry van Dyke, D.D., LL.D., Princeton University.
The Right Rev. William Lawrence, D.D., LL.D., representing Durham University, Eng.
The Rev. Professor George William Knox, D.D., LL.D., Union Theological Seminary.
J. Pierpont Morgan, LL.D.
The Hon. Seth Low, LL.D., Director of Union Theological Seminary.
The Rev. President Howard S. Bliss, D.D., Syrian Protestant College, Beirût.
The Rev. Dean Edward L. Curtis, Ph.D., D.D., Yale University.
President Jacob Gould Schurman, Sc.D., LL.D., Cornell University.

* Unavoidably absent.

The Rev. President ROBERT W. FALCONER, D.D., LL.D., University of Toronto.
Dean JAMES E. RUSSELL, PH.D., LL.D., Teachers College, Columbia University.
The Rev. Principal HOLLIS B. FRISSELL, D.D., LL.D., Hampton Institute.
The Rev. Professor JOHN CHARLES ROPER, D.D., representing Oxford University.
The Rev. Professor DUNCAN B. MACDONALD, D.D., representing Glasgow University.

The other guests were seated at small tables which were tastefully decorated. Souvenir pamphlets containing pictures and a description of the new buildings were furnished to each of the guests. Grace was said by the Reverend James D. Moffat, D.D., LL.D., President of Washington and Jefferson College. At a quarter past nine promptly the meeting was called to order by the presiding officer, Dr. Robert Curtis Ogden, who welcomed the delegates and guests present in fitting words, and read a letter from the President of the United States, the Honorable William H. Taft, LL.D., in which he expressed regret at his inability to be present.

Dr. Ogden then introduced the speakers of the evening, who responded to the following toasts:

President NICHOLAS MURRAY BUTLER, PH.D., LL.D. Our Neighbors.
The Right Reverend DAVID H. GREER, D.D., LL.D. The City.
The Reverend GEORGE ALEXANDER, D.D. The World.
The Rev. Professor EDWARD C. MOORE, D.D. The University.
The Right Reverend WILLIAM LAWRENCE, D.D., LL.D. Our Friends across the Sea.
The Rev. Professor GEORGE WILLIAM KNOX, D.D., LL.D. The Seminary.
The Rev. President JAMES G. K. McCLURE, D.D. Sister Seminaries.
The Rev. President WILLIAM H. P. FAUNCE, D.D., LL.D., The Spirit of Service.
The Rev. President FRANCIS BROWN, D.D., LL.D. Retrospect and Prospect.

The speaking concluded promptly at eleven o'clock, and Dr. Ogden dismissed the audience with the words: "Ladies and Gentlemen, good night."

III

THE INSTITUTIONS REPRESENTED

THE INSTITUTIONS REPRESENTED

The following Institutions, arranged in the order of foundation, were represented by the Delegates named:

THE UNIVERSITY OF OXFORD, the Rev. Professor J. CHARLES ROPER, D.D.

THE UNIVERSITY OF ST. ANDREWS, ANDREW CARNEGIE, LL.D.

GLASGOW UNIVERSITY, the Rev. Professor DUNCAN B. MACDONALD, D.D.

THE UNIVERSITY OF MARBURG, the Rev. Professor W. W. ROCKWELL, LIC.TH. (Marburg).

HARVARD UNIVERSITY, the Rev. Professor EDWARD C. MOORE, PH.D., D.D.

YALE UNIVERSITY, the Rev. Dean EDWARD L. CURTIS, PH.D., D.D., the Rev. JAMES W. COOPER, D.D.

YALE DIVINITY SCHOOL, the Rev. Professor HENRY H. TWEEDY, M.A.

THE UNIVERSITY OF PENNSYLVANIA, the Rev. Professor J. A. MONTGOMERY, PH.D., S.T.D.

COLUMBIA UNIVERSITY, President NICHOLAS MURRAY BUTLER, PH.D., LL.D., LITT.D., the Right Rev. DAVID H. GREER, D.D., LL.D., Professor JOHN W. BURGESS, PH.D., LL.D.

BROWN UNIVERSITY, the Rev. President W. H. P. FAUNCE, D.D., LL.D.

DARTMOUTH COLLEGE, CHARLES F. MATHEWSON, LL.B., A.M.

RUTGERS COLLEGE, the Rev. Professor GEORGE H. PAYSON, D.D.

THE THEOLOGICAL SEMINARY OF THE REFORMED CHURCH IN AMERICA, the Rev. Professor EDWARD P. JOHNSON, D.D.

THE UNIVERSITY OF GEORGIA, GEORGE FOSTER PEABODY, LL.D.

WILLIAMS COLLEGE, President HARRY A. GARFIELD, LL.D.

BOWDOIN COLLEGE, General THOMAS H. HUBBARD, LL.D.

UNION UNIVERSITY, the Rev. President CHARLES A. RICHMOND, D.D., LL.D.

MIDDLEBURY COLLEGE, the Rev. President JOHN M. THOMAS, D.D.

WASHINGTON AND JEFFERSON COLLEGE, the Rev. President JAMES D. MOFFAT, D.D., LL.D.

ANDOVER THEOLOGICAL SEMINARY, the Rev. President ALBERT PARKER FITCH, D.D., the Rev. CHARLES L. NOYES, D.D.

MORAVIAN COLLEGE, the Rev. President AUGUSTUS SCHULTZE, D.D., L.H.D.

HAMILTON COLLEGE, the Rev. ROBERT G. MCGREGOR, B.D.

BANGOR THEOLOGICAL SEMINARY, the Rev. Professor W. J. MOULTON, PH.D., D.D.

THE GENERAL THEOLOGICAL SEMINARY, the Rev. Professor HERBERT M. DENSLOW, D.D.

THE UNIVERSITY OF PITTSBURGH, the Rev. Chancellor S. B. MCCORMICK, D.D., LL.D., the Rev. S. B. LINHART, D.D.

AUBURN THEOLOGICAL SEMINARY, the Rev. Professor ARTHUR S. HOYT, D.D.

MCGILL UNIVERSITY, Principal WILLIAM PETERSON, LL.D., C.M.G.

TRINITY COLLEGE (Hartford, Conn.) the Rev. PHILIP COOK.

NEWTON THEOLOGICAL INSTITUTION, the Rev. President GEORGE E. HORR, D.D.

THE THEOLOGICAL SEMINARY OF THE REFORMED CHURCH IN UNITED STATES, Lancaster, Pennsylvania, the Rev. President JOHN C. BOWMAN, D.D.

WESTERN THEOLOGICAL SEMINARY, Pittsburg, Pennsylvania, the Rev. President JAMES A. KELSO, PH.D., D.D., the Rev. Professor D. SCHLEY SCHAFF, D.D.

WESTERN RESERVE UNIVERSITY, the Rev. Professor ARTHUR C. MCGIFFERT, PH.D., D.D.

THE UNIVERSITY OF TORONTO, President ROBERT W. FALCONER, D.D., LL.D.

HANOVER COLLEGE, the Rev. JOHN C. PALMER, D.D.

ILLINOIS COLLEGE, the Rev. THOMAS W. SMITH, D.D.

NEW YORK UNIVERSITY, Professor JOHN H. MACCRACKEN, PH.D., LL.D, Dean D. W. HERING, PH.D., LL.D., Dean FRANCIS H. STODDARD, PH.D.

WESLEYAN UNIVERSITY, Professor ANDREW C. ARMSTRONG, PH.D.

LAFAYETTE COLLEGE, Professor WILLIAM B. OWEN, PH.D.

PENNSYLVANIA COLLEGE, the Rev. JAMES B. REMENSNYDER, D.D., LL.D.

HAVERFORD COLLEGE, President ISAAC SHARPLESS, LL.D.

THE UNIVERSITY OF DURHAM, (England), the Right Rev. WILLIAM LAWRENCE, D.D., LL.D., D.C.L.

HARTFORD THEOLOGICAL SEMINARY, the Rev. Professor E. K. MITCHELL, D.D.
WABASH COLLEGE, the Rev. ARTHUR J. BROWN, D.D.
ALFRED UNIVERSITY, the Rev. Professor WILLIAM C. WHITFORD, D.D.
MOUNT HOLYOKE COLLEGE, President MARY E. WOOLLEY, D.LITT., Professor SAMUEL P. HAYES, PH.D.
THE UNIVERSITY OF MISSOURI, Professor CASSIUS J. KEYSER, PH.D.
OHIO WESLEYAN UNIVERSITY, EDWARD J. WHEELER, M.A., LITT.D.
MEADVILLE THEOLOGICAL SCHOOL, the Rev. President F. C. SOUTHWORTH, M.A., S.T.B.
WESTMINSTER COLLEGE, (Cambridge, England), the Rev. G. A. JOHNSTON ROSS, M.A.
COLGATE UNIVERSITY, the Rev. Dean W. H. ALLISON, PH.D.
KNOX COLLEGE—Toronto, the Rev. Principal ALFRED GANDIER, D.D.
MOUNT UNION COLLEGE, President W. H. MCMASTER, D.D.
EARLHAM COLLEGE, the Rev. ROBERT E. PRETLOW, M.A.
LAWRENCE COLLEGE, the Rev. President BRADFORD P. RAYMOND, D.D., LL.D.
THE COLLEGE OF THE CITY OF NEW YORK, Professor FITZGERALD TISDALL, PH.D.
OBERLIN COLLEGE, the Rev. C. J. RYDER, D.D.
ROCHESTER THEOLOGICAL SEMINARY, the Rev. President A. H. STRONG, D.D., LL.D.
NORTHWESTERN UNIVERSITY, CHARLES HARVEY FAHS, B.D., the Rev. GEORGE MOONEY, A.B., the Rev. THOMAS NICHOLSON, D.D., LL.D.
VICTORIA UNIVERSITY OF MANCHESTER, ENGLAND, President NICHOLAS MURRAY BUTLER, PH.D., LL.D., D.LITT.
TRINITY COLLEGE, Durham, North Carolina, Professor GEORGE B. PEGRAM, PH.D.
TUFTS COLLEGE, the Rev. FRANK OLIVER HALL, D.D.
BERKELEY DIVINITY SCHOOL, the Rev. Professor WILLIAM PALMER LADD, B.D.
CHICAGO THEOLOGICAL SEMINARY, the Rev. President OZORA S. DAVIS, D.D.
BEREA COLLEGE, the Rev. President WILLIAM G. FROST, D.D., LL.D.
HILLSDALE COLLEGE, the Rev. RIVINGTON D. LORD, D.D.
THE PROTESTANT EPISCOPAL DIVINITY SCHOOL OF PHILADELPHIA, the Rev. Professor LUCIEN M. ROBINSON, D.D.

McCormick Theological Seminary, the Rev. President James G. K. McClure, D.D., LL.D.
Vassar College, the Rev. President James M. Taylor, D.D., LL.D.
The University of Washington, Professor A. H. Yoder.
The Syrian Protestant College, Beirût, Syria, the Rev. President Howard S. Bliss, D.D.
The German Presbyterian Theological School of the Northwest, Dubuque, Iowa, the Rev. Professor Daniel Grieder, D.D.
The Lutheran Theological Seminary, Mount Airy, Philadelphia, the Rev. Luther D. Reed, M.A.
Robert College (Constantinople), the Rev. Edward B. Coe, D.D.
Swarthmore College, Vice-President George A. Hoadley, LL.D.
Cornell University, President Jacob Gould Schurman, LL.D.
Lehigh University, President Henry S. Drinker, LL.D., the Right Rev. Ethelbert Talbot, D.D., LL.D.
Carleton College, the Rev. Arcturus Z. Conrad, Ph.D., D.D.
Drew Theological Seminary, the Rev. Professor R. W. Rogers, Ph.D., D.D., LL.D.
The University of Wooster, the Rev. Professor Chalmers Martin, D.D.
Atlanta University, the Rev. President Edward Twitchell Ware.
Crozer Theological Seminary, the Rev. Professor Spenser B. Meeser, D.D.
The Episcopal Theological School of Cambridge, the Very Rev. Dean George Hodges, D.D., D.C.L.
Fisk University, the Rev. President George A. Gates, D.D., Professor Warren G. Waterman, M.A.
Howard University, the Rev. President Wilbur P. Thirkield, D.D., LL.D.
Iowa College, Professor George M. Whicher, Litt.D.
The University of Illinois, Edward L. Abbott, B.S.
Hampton Normal and Agricultural Institute, the Rev. Principal Hollis B. Frissell, D.D., LL.D.
Boston University, the Rev. William I. Haven, D.D.
German Theological School of Newark, New Jersey, the Rev. Professor Henry J. Weber, Ph.D., D.D.

URSINUS COLLEGE, the Rev. President A. EDWIN KEIGWIN, D.D.
DRURY COLLEGE, the Rev. W. L. SCHMALHORST.
COLORADO COLLEGE, the Rev. President WILLIAM F. SLOCUM, D.D., LL.D.
PURDUE UNIVERSITY, DANIEL RALPH LUCAS, M.D.
THE STATE UNIVERSITY OF IOWA, JOHN G. BOWMAN, M.A.
DOSHISHA COLLEGE, the Rev. President TASUKU HARADA, LL.D.
PARK COLLEGE, the Rev. CLELAND B. MCAFEE, D.D.
SMITH COLLEGE, Professor HARRY N. GARDINER, M.A.
WELLESLEY COLLEGE, Professor ALICE VAN VECHTEN BROWN.
JOHNS HOPKINS UNIVERSITY, the Rev. Dean E. H. GRIFFIN, D.D., LL.D.
WASEDA UNIVERSITY, Professor K. ASAKAWA, PH.D.
HURON COLLEGE, the Rev. President CALVIN H. FRENCH, D.D.
THE UNIVERSITY OF NORTH DAKOTA, MAXWELL M. UPSON, B.A.
TEMPLE UNIVERSITY, the Rev. Dean WALTER B. SHUMWAY, D.D.
BRYN MAWR COLLEGE, President M. CAREY THOMAS, LL.D.
THE MEMORIAL THEOLOGICAL SEMINARY, Saharanpur, India, the Rev. Professor H. C. DELTE, M.A.
CANTON CHRISTIAN COLLEGE, Mr. W. HENRY GRANT.
THE JEWISH THEOLOGICAL SEMINARY OF AMERICA, Professor ISRAEL FRIEDLÄNDER, PH.D.
MANSFIELD COLLEGE, Oxford, England, the Rev. AMORY H. BRADFORD, D.D.
NORTH JAPAN COLLEGE, Sendai, Japan, Professor TEIZABURO DEMURA, M.A.
CLARK UNIVERSITY, President EDMUND C. SANFORD, PH.D., Sc.D.
TEACHERS COLLEGE (Columbia University), Dean JAMES E. RUSSELL, PH.D., LL.D.
POMONA COLLEGE, the Rev. MILTON WITTLER, B.D.
BARNARD COLLEGE, Provost WILLIAM T. BREWSTER, M.A., SILAS B. BROWNELL, LL.D.
NORTH CHINA UNION COLLEGE, the Rev. ARTHUR H. SMITH, D.D.
LELAND STANFORD JR., UNIVERSITY, Professor R. L. WILBUR, M.A., M.D.
MORNINGSIDE COLLEGE, FRED J. SEAVER, PH.D.

ALLAHABAD CHRISTIAN COLLEGE, CHARLES D. THOMPSON, JR.
CENTRAL THEOLOGICAL SEMINARY, the Rev. Professor JAMES I. GOOD, D.D.

Courteous messages of regret came from other institutions, some of which sent also congratulatory addresses, which were received with appreciation.

IV

THE DEDICATION SERMON

THE DEDICATION SERMON

By the Reverend Henry Sloane Coffin, D.D.

Psalm lxi, 5.
"Thou hast given me the heritage of those that fear thy name."

Our first thought, as we set apart these stately and graceful buildings to their use for the Kingdom of God, is naturally of those to whose large faith and generous thought we owe both the plan for the enlargement of this Seminary's work and the means for its accomplishment. We recall with reverent and grateful affection the late President of the Faculty, Charles Cuthbert Hall, who dreamt dreams of the destiny possible to this institution upon this commanding site at the great academic center of the metropolis of the continent; the Christian men of affairs in our Board of Directors, who shared his vision and made possible its achievement upon a scale surpassing even his sanguine hope, such men as John Crosby Brown and Morris K. Jesup; and in particular that broad-minded, truth-loving, far-seeing business man, whose memory this chapel records, D. Willis James, the Greatheart in the company of those who in recent years have with signal wisdom, assurance and devotion guided this school of sacred learning. Of them we may say as we look about upon that which they planned, but were not permitted to see completed, "These all died in faith, not having received these promises, but having seen them and greeted them from afar." We cannot but feel that they commit to us very wistfully and very trustingly this heavy responsibility, the weight of which they appreciate, because they carried it in anticipation. And we, as we accept it from God so directly through them, are keenly sensible that their consecration in planning and providing has already given its solemn dedication to that which we are now setting apart to its intended use. The dedication comes with the gift itself, as we say gratefully, "Thou hast given us the heritage of those that fear thy name."

And with these who conceived and prepared for these

impressive buildings we would couple in our thankful remembrance the illustrious rôle of teachers, who in the past have won distinction for this Seminary by their scholarship, the pastors and missionaries who have gone from its halls to bring honor to its name by their efficient service of the Church of Christ, and the ministers and laymen, who with singular freedom from denominational prejudice and untrammeled by traditionalism, with faith in the living God, loyalty to Jesus Christ, and seeking to be as inclusive in their sympathy as He, have shaped its policy, supplied its endowments, directed its affairs and moulded its spirit. It has been theirs to command for this institution that trust and attachment manifestly evidenced in this incomparable equipment for its work. It is ours—and how weighty the obligation!—to deserve what it has been theirs to secure.

We are dedicating this costly plant to the preparation of preachers and teachers of religion. Religion comes to every man, no matter how independent an investigator he may be in his fellowship with the Invisible, as an inheritance. It is significant that two of our evangelists in presenting the biography of the world's most startling religious Innovator, its most original and self-reliant Man of faith, supply us with His genealogy, as though His unique convictions were inexplicable and unintelligible apart from their antecedents in a long succession of believers. This Seminary has been called in the providence of God to stand for the right and the duty of each generation to think its own thought of the Most High. But this by no means implies our want of reverence for those who have preceded us in the life of faith. It is not the imitative followers of adventurous leaders who are in closest sympathy with them, but the pioneers who gratefully acknowledge the bounds which their precursors reached, and instead of remaining within them set out from them to add to the territory already attained. The God we trust has been man's old, old home. There can be nothing strictly new in our intercourse with Him. Every emotion we feel in His presence, every thought of Him that comes to our minds, every word we utter of praise or petition, every rite we perform in worship, every task to which we set ourselves as our Father's business, has a long history behind it. God, even with His unsearchable riches, would not mean so much to us were it not that into their fellowship with Him, as into their permanent home, centuries of believing men and women have put their personalities.

"The souls of many thousand years
Have laid up here their toils and fears
And all the agonies of their pain."

Religion, no doubt, means to every man a private understanding between himself and God. He is conscious of following no precedent as he places himself in the everlasting arms. He is not aware that he is obeying an age-long tradition when he responds to the voice of God in his conscience. He flies to Him and obeys Him spontaneously, as though God and he had been made for each other, and suddenly he recognized the affinity. But when he comes to reflect upon his private fellowship with the Father he discovers that he has entered a great household of faith. The impulse that drove him to an unseen Friend and the conscience that spoke to him with commanding authority have behind them a far-stretching heredity. The confession of his weakness and failure and sin which he is pouring into the divine ear seems an echo that comes sounding from every century of the voices of the contrite in heart. His aspiration which rises towards godlikeness in temper and sympathy and usefulness appears as the outbreathing through him of the souls of the upreaching of every generation. His consecration to the kingdom of love is an ancient fire that has blazed in the spirits of untold thousands since time began. His timid knock at the door of the divine heart for companionship has admitted him to a thronged presence, where men out of every kindred and tongue and era stand before God. The divine voice that seemed to whisper its confidential secret in his ear now sounds as the voice of many waters, a great harmony of all the heavenly tones that have fallen on the ears of men from the beginning. Paul uses a bold but true phrase when he speaks of "the riches of the glory of God's inheritance in the saints." There is a genuine sense in which God Himself has more to offer us because of His acquisitions in the past from all who have served Him and are now with Him abidingly. Our first exclamation when we come into the secret place of the Most High may be, "O God, Thou art my God." But our next will be: "Lord, Thou hast been our dwelling place in all generations." "Thou hast given me the heritage of those that fear Thy name."

There are some who would challenge our right to place this theological seminary beside institutions where sciences like mathematics and chemistry and astronomy are studied. Theology is not to them a science because it does not deal with actual fact. There is no reality they say corresponding to the name we reverence. Faith in God is an hallucination destined to become as obsolete as the belief in ghosts and witches. Religion should be studied as part of pathology in a course in a medical school that deals with nervous disorders, or as an historical curiosity, as we examine the superstitions of savages. But in setting this school of theology side by side with these other scientific institutions we claim that we deal with reality as truly as they. "We know Whom we have believed." The invisible God is as genuine a fact of human experience as men and things, although we apprehend Him by faith and not by sight. Like other sciences, theology tests and criticizes its conclusions, and grows more clear and precise from age to age. Its data are given, as are all other scientific data, through the experiences of men, primarily the experiences of the living—for we are in touch with the living God—but also, and often far more richly, through the experiences of the religiously gifted of the past, the seers of all time. It is the discoveries of their souls in God, discoveries confirmed by similar experiences of our own, which give us the name we fear. Ten thousand times ten thousand of every race and condition have been in Christ before us, and these all have had witness borne to them through their faith. Their witness is evidence which we are not afraid to submit to the most rigorous tests. The forms in which they bore their testimony may be open to correction and improvement, but the testimony itself is unimpeachable. "They looked unto Him and were radiant." They discovered, as it were, a vast new continent. They explored and chartered Him who is invisible. They mined unsearchable riches of comfort and strength in God. They reaped harvests of peace and joy from fellowship with Him. They have been enraptured with prospects of surpassing beauty in the character of the Altogether Lovely. They have emigrated to Him and exchanged the ideals and sympathies and interests of the world about them for the mind and heart and purpose of God, and He has been the home of their spirits while they moved freely in the life of earth. The name they fear is the interpretation of their experience, their description of what God has been to them. And that name they pass on to us as their most precious bequest.

The word in our text which needs most emphasis to-day is the word "name." There is so much anonymous religion among us. Men devote themselves to investigations of various sets of facts, to the invention of all sorts of appliances, to social justice, to economic readjustment, to political reform, to art, to crusades against disease and vice, with a consecration that is essentially religious. In every sphere of life one finds altars to an unknown God. The devotees of personal integrity and public rightousness, the zealots for sympathy and service are legion. And for all this we cannot be too grateful. But relatively few of the followers of truth and right, beauty and love, are aware that through these they are in fellowship with the Lord of heaven and earth, the God and Father of us all. We should impress our ancestors as extremely undevout. They might call us irreligious. And in part they would be justified. One cannot imagine our contemporaries establishing a day of public thanksgiving to God. That custom remains with us as a survival from an era when men in general took God far more seriously than do we. Ours is not an age of public or family or personal prayer. Men do not ask themselves how they stand with God. Pure religion and undefiled is, for us, to visit the fatherless and widows in their affliction and to keep oneself unspotted from the world, but we forget that James wrote, "Pure religion and undefiled before our God and Father." We insist that it is required of us "to do justly and to love mercy," but we seldom finish the sentence, "to walk humbly with thy God." We assent to the saying that whatever we do to the least of Christ's brethren we do to Him, but we are not often conscious of direct intercourse between ourselves and Him in the service of men. Our sense of social responsibility is strong, but we have little sense of personal accountability to God. Not many men give us the impression of being intimate with the Most High, "far ben," as the Scotch say, His close friends and companions.

It would be very easy and pleasant, although certainly not novel, to point out the advances we have made upon those who bequeathed us their convictions. The founders of this institution would probably admit that we were trying to apply Christianity to many relationships of life which they had overlooked. The attempt seriously to embody the mind of Christ in business ethics, in international affairs, in the treatment of the criminal, in every phase of our complex social existence, commands far more interest than in their day. One is sure, however, in reading the charter of this institution that with all this modern broadening of the scope of our religious responsibility our founders would have been in complete accord. But in this development we must admit that there have been some, perhaps unavoidable, losses. We have lost in our thoughtfulness of God. His universe is so fascinating and absorbing that we seem to have no surplus attention to devote to Him. We have lost in reverence. The Old Testament phrase " them that fear Thy name" seems scarcely applicable to our religious experience. We have lost the tone of authority which conscience had when men connected it directly with Him that sitteth upon the throne. And above all we have lost that definite consciousness of our personal relationship with God, which comes very near to being the essence of vital religion. Indeed, there is much Christianity which it would not be wholly false to describe as godless. There are many men who share the humanitarian attitude of Jesus, who are in sympathy with His ethical ideals, who cherish His social hopes, but who part company with Him in that which was with Him fundamental—His sonship with God.

They, whose legatees you and I are, were no worshippers of an unnamed Deity. They knew Him far too personally for that. He was the God and Father of Jesus Christ, the God who revealed Himself to holy men of old and is still revealing Himself to holy men to-day, the God who became entirely frank with His children when His Word became flesh and dwelt among us, and so gave us God's own name for Himself:

" Jesus, name of wondrous love,
Human name of God above."

Jesus of Nazareth was for them, as He is for us, God's Self-disclosure in a human life, " God's God in the mind of man."

One may say without exaggeration that all the efforts of the scholars who gave this Seminary its reputation in days gone by, and all the struggles for truth and liberty in which it has engaged, were motived by the desire to set forth more clearly Jesus Christ as the only and final name for God. This was the impulse which led its teachers of a past generation to modify their inherited Calvinism, and which has influenced its more recent scholars in their Biblical criticism and their restatement of theology in terms of the social purpose of Jesus—the Kingdom of God. Many good people have not understood them, and have been led to criticize and oppose, when could they but have known their motive, they would have been in heartiest sympathy with them. Such misunderstandings are pathetically inevitable in all advances of thought. The interest in Jesus Christ we inherit is in Him as the name, the revelation of God. We give Him all our loyalty, all our trust, all our consecration, all our worship, and are not idolaters, because He is for us the image of the invisible God. When we name Him, we do not think merely of One who lived in the past, but of the living God, His God and Father, of whom He is the likeness and to whom He is the way.

The task to which those whose heritage is this conviction must set themselves to-day is the interpretation to men by Jesus of that which they are seeking with such religious devotion anonymously. "What ye worship in ignorance, this I set forth unto you—the God that made the world and all things therein, He being Lord of heaven and earth, is our Father disclosed in Jesus Christ, His Son." We must make them feel that in investigating truth, they are discovering the mind of the All-wise, whose treasures of wisdom and knowledge for life are accessible in Christ; that in shouldering social obligations they are bearing burdens which rest on the heart of One who unceasingly and unsparingly gives Himself to be God and Father to everybody, as Jesus gave Himself to be everyone's Friend; that in attempting economic readjustments by which none shall waste and none shall want, they are fulfilling His will in whose household there is bread enough and to spare, and that in the solution of their complex problems they can draw on His wisdom and sympathy extended in Jesus; that in working for human health and happiness, they have His co-operation whose attitude towards pain and misery is manifest in Him who Himself took our infirmities and bore our diseases, and willed that His joy should be in us and that our joy should be made full; that in seeking to redeem the worthless into useful men and women, and to regenerate a selfish world into a "realm where the air we breathe is love," they are co-workers of Him whose eternal purpose is the heavenly social order Jesus proclaimed and whose nature is the redeeming love commended to a sinning world on Calvary. The heritage of which we, with the Church universal, are custodians, and which it is ours to give to all men, is fellowship with God through Jesus Christ in seeking His kingdom and His righteousness.

It is significant that the most noticeable and the most beautiful of this group of buildings is not that which contains the library or the lecture rooms, but the chapel. This Seminary exists to train men to be skilful workmen in a most, surely in the most, difficult of callings—the inspiration of lives with the Spirit of God. In their equipment we deem the primary requisite not knowledge of methods of work, not familiarity with the best religious thought of others, past or present, but personal acquaintance with God Himself. Before all they must be "men of God." And as the center of this institution's life on its new site, as on its old, we dedicate a house of prayer.

That which claims the first attention of all who enter here is yonder window. It symbolizes two great sacraments. The one is the sacrament of responsibility. "Go ye into all the world and make disciples of all the nations." It reminds us that the Church's task is the transformation of an entire world into the kingdom of love, the remodeling of every institution and the redemption of every man, woman and child, until society is divine and every individual Christlike. And such responsibility is a sacrament. It is when men are captivated by this vision and feel themselves committed to this labor that they realize how desirable, how indispensable God is.

"Ere earth gain her heavenly best a God must mingle in the game."

The other is the sacrament of memory. The window commemorates a Christian who was a splendid type of the God-fearing man this Seminary would have its graduates seek to produce by their ministry; and it portrays in symbolical figures the Church of the past and above all its Lord and ours. As the light streams through those figured panes into our faces, so through the memories of the saints, and supremely of the King of saints, God reveals to us His name. There is the type of religion for which this Seminary stands—a whole world for which to feel responsible, and the God disclosed in Jesus Christ and all His followers with whom to serve it. This responsibility and these memories are our inheritance, the heritage of those that fear God's name.

V

THE ADDRESSES AT THE STUDENT MEETING

1 Historical Address by the Reverend Professor William Adams Brown, PH.D., D.D.

2 Address by President Jacob Gould Schurman, LL.D., "Some Elements of Religious Progress."

I.

Historical Address

By the Reverend Professor William Adams Brown, PH.D., D.D.

I have been asked to tell you as much of the history of the Seminary as it is possible to crowd into thirty minutes. I am sure you will feel for me. If, in my life as a teacher, I have ever been lacking in sympathy with any of you, my fellow students, as you have tried to compress the wisdom of a lifetime into the rapidly-vanishing minutes of an examination hour, I repent now in dust and ashes. On my table at home lies a paper which represents my final effort at condensation. It would take me just an hour and fifteen minutes to read it. Our beloved President, masking under his gentle mien an inexorable resolution, refuses to allow me five minutes more. What am I to do?

What can I do but what I have done; leave my paper at home and start afresh? What I bring to you to-night is not a history of the Seminary, but the impression which has been left on my mind as I have tried to relive it.

Every one of us has two lives, an outer and an inner. The former is made up of event and incident, and the complete record of it would fill many volumes; the latter is a quality of spirit, and a half hour spent alone over the fire may suffice for the revelation of the best we have. It is with institutions as it is with men. They are spirit as well as body, and it is the spirit that counts. Bear with me, then, as I try to interpret to you the spirit of the Seminary as it has revealed itself to me in my communion with the memories of the past.

The first impression that I have carried away is one of inner consistency. The story is all of a piece. Seventy-five years ago nine gentlemen met in the study of Mr. Knowles Taylor, a prominent New York layman, to consider the expediency of establishing a theological seminary in the City of

New York. Five of the nine were laymen. All were men eminent in their various callings and professions. All were devoted, heart and soul, to the cause of missions, home and foreign, and many of them were officers or active workers in the great missionary societies.

These men felt the need of a training school for the Christian ministry, different in kind from any which was then in existence. The seminaries with which they were familiar failed to satisfy them at three points. In the first place, they were under ecclesiastical control; in the second place, the training which they gave was narrow; in the third place, they were remote from the great centres of human life. The men who founded Union believed that there was room for something different, and the ideal which animated them they have put into words which no Union Seminary man will ever forget.

I will not repeat here the famous preamble, which is the charter of our liberties. It is enough to remind you of its salient points, so far as they are necessary for the understanding of the history that followed.

In the first place, the founders expressed their belief that a great city furnishes peculiar facilities and advantages for conducting theological education.

In the second place, while providing for instruction in the doctrine and discipline of the Presbyterian Church, of which they were members, they declared their purpose to furnish the means of a full and thorough education in all the subjects taught in the best theological seminaries in this and other countries.

In the third place, they emphasized the importance of practical training for an efficient ministry. They believed that it was not enough to be pious and scholarly; one must know how to express his faith and to apply his knowledge in action. Accordingly, they proposed that their students identify themselves with the various churches of the city, actively engage in their services and become familiar with all the benevolent efforts of the city and of the time.

In the fourth place, they proposed to train men not only for the Christian ministry, but for every form of Christian service, whether educational, philanthropic or religious.

Finally, they wished to provide an institution of truly catholic spirit, or, in other words, to use their own memorable language, one " around which all men of moderate views and feelings who desire to live free from party strife and to stand aloof from all extremes of doctrinal speculation, practical radicalism and ecclesiastical domination, may cordially and affectionately rally."

Contact with life in its intensest form, the most thorough training possible, practical discipline gained through repeated experiment, a wide outlook and a catholic sympathy, a liberty safeguarded against the dangers of license, whether on the side of thought or practice, by devotion to a great cause:—such were the ideals of the founders for the institution they created. We, their descendants, surveying their work after the lapse of three quarters of a century, find nothing either to add or to take away.

No doubt there were ups and downs in the history. We do not always see things with equal clearness, and we are not always equally true to what we see. Yet, on the whole, I repeat, the impression produced is one of singular consistency. What Union Seminary was to the mind of its founders, that it is to us, their descendants, to-day.

The story of the outer life falls into five chapters. First, the days of struggle and weakness, from 1835 to 1852; secondly, the period of reconstruction, financial and educational, from 1852 to the reunion of the old and new schools in 1870; thirdly, the period of enlarging activity and growing usefulness, including the presidency of William Adams, from 1873 to 1880, and culminating in the removal of the Seminary to its new site on Lenox Hill in 1884. Fourthly, the period of storm and stress, marked by the veto of Dr. Briggs' transfer by the General Assembly in 1891, the resumption by the Seminary in 1892 of the independence which it had surrendered in 1870, and the trials of Dr. Briggs and of Dr. McGiffert, and ending with the alteration of the terms of subscription in 1904. Finally, the new era of opportunity and service, in the dawn of which we stand to-day: 1835 to 1852; 1852 to 1870; 1870 to 1884; 1884 to 1904; 1904 to the present—these are the outward landmarks. What they mean for the inner life of the institution we have now to consider.

What then is this spirit of Union, of which we love to speak? First of all, it is a spirit of confidence in the truth. If anything may be said to be characteristic of the Seminary it is this. The founders were, with a single exception, New School men, and this is only another way of saying that they were confirmed optimists. Their differences with the Old School men were not so much theological as ecclesiastical and practical. They believed that God was in his Heaven, and therefore that all was well with His world. It was not that they were more radical in their theology, but that they were more hopeful in spirit. They believed that the truth was able to take care of itself, and were eager to co-operate in practical effort with every one who shared this faith. Those whom they associated with them were men of like mind with themselves, and the new Seminary became almost from its birth the organ of the New School and the training school of its ministers in the new era of independence which the disruption of 1837 forced upon it.

A single instance will illustrate what I mean. When Henry B. Smith came to the Seminary in 1850 he was fresh from New England, and what was still more dangerous, only four years away from Germany. In his inaugural address at Andover a few years before, he had paid a glowing tribute to Schleiermacher as the great German theologian, who first in modern times led his fellow countrymen back to the feet of Christ. It was not strange that a man of such a type should be looked upon askance in Presbyterian circles. It seems that some of his own colleagues had their doubts.

Dr. Smith thus describes a conversation which he had with Dr. White, his colleague in the Chair of Systematic Theology, just before he came to the Seminary.

"Last evening I spent wholly till eleven o'clock and after with Dr. White talking over the whole Seminary and matters thereto belonging. He was rather curious about some of my theological opinions, and we got into a discussion of two hours on the person of Christ, in which he claimed that I advocated something inconsistent with the Catechism, and I claimed that he taught what was against the Catechism, which was rather a hard saying against an old-established professor of theology. However, it was all very well and kind on both sides, and did not prevent his urging my coming here."

"It was all very well and kind on both sides, and did not prevent his urging my coming here." Here speaks the spirit of Union; mutual confidence consistent with the recognition of individual differences. So may it ever be. God forbid that the day shall ever come when all the members of the Union Seminary faculty shall be men of one type, however excellent that type may be.

Next in the order of my impressions is that of thoroughness of preparation. The men who founded Union Seminary were men of affairs, and they believed in training. They thought the best training possible was none too good for a minister of Jesus Christ. They believed in training in theory as well as training in practice, important as they regarded the latter, and strenuously as they insisted upon it. In the darkest days of the institution, when the Seminary was practically bankrupt, they invested $5,000 in the Van Ess Library, a sum more than half as great as that paid for the site of the building. They knew that a seminary without books was a contradiction in terms, and they were determined that Union should have the best that could be obtained, whatever the cost.

The spirit of the founders was the spirit of the professors. I wish I had the time to read the letter written by Dr. Robinson when he accepted his appointment to the Chair of Biblical Literature. It was no light matter, I can tell you, to study under this insatiable scholar.

" To understand the Bible," he tells us, "the student must know all about the Bible. It is not a mere smattering of Greek and Hebrew, not the mere ability to consult a text in the original Scriptures, that can qualify him to be a correct interpreter of the word of life. He must be thoroughly furnished for his work if he be expected to do his work well."

And then he goes on to enumerate the particulars which fall within the department as he understands it.

" To it properly belong full courses of instruction in the Hebrew, Greek and Chaldee languages, and also as auxiliaries in the Syriac, Arabic and other minor dialects; in Biblical Introduction, or the history of the Bible as a whole and its various parts, its writers, its manuscripts, editions, etc.; in Biblical Criticism, or the History and condition of the text; in Biblical Hermeneutics, or the theory and principles of Interpretation; in Biblical Exegesis or the practical application of those principles to the study and interpretation of the sacred books; in Biblical Antiquities; and further, a separate consideration of the version of the Seventy as a chief source of illustration for both the Old and New Testaments."

This was written in 1837. Even our own beloved Dr. Briggs, from his high tower of theological encyclopædia surveying the whole field of human knowledge, could find little to add to such a program.

New subjects have taken their place in the Seminary curriculum, but the old spirit lives on. If sometimes in our zeal we younger men are tempted to ask of our students more than we ought, you must remember the training we have ourselves received. To those who have studied under Dr. Briggs, Edward Robinson professor in fact as well as in name, and the teachers whom he has trained, lack of thoroughness is not an intellectual failing, it is a moral fault. We cannot help this feeling. It is bred in our bones. We have drunk it in from the mother who has nurtured us. We owe it to ourselves; we owe it to our fellowmen; we owe it to our Master, to learn all that we can learn, that we may be able to do all that we can do.

With confidence in the truth and thoroughness of training went courage in the defense of the right. This is my third impression. Twice in its history the Seminary has faced a crisis which would have daunted men of less heroic mould. From each it has emerged triumphant. The first was financial. It met the Seminary on the threshold of its history before it had had time to take root in the new soil. The founders met for the first time in 1835. Two years later the panic of 1837 swept over the country, carrying down with it many of those on whose support they had relied. Many of the subscriptions, which had been made in good faith, could not be collected. The original plans which contemplated houses for the professors had to be abandoned. The property was heavily mortgaged, the salaries of the professors were often months in arrears, and they were reduced to every shift to keep body and soul together.

But they never faltered for a moment. The darker grew the outlook, "the more hopeful, even brilliant" it seemed to them. The words are not my own, but those of Mr. Charles Butler, *clarum et venerabile nomen*,—long time our honored President, himself one of the founders and a participant of the vicissitudes of those early days. "I can recall in memory," he says, "but cannot describe the feeling that was reflected on the countenances of the members when called together to consider what could be done to meet the impending exigencies. These meetings were generally attended by the professors as well and were always opened and closed with prayer." Thus began a feature of the Seminary life which has been characteristic ever since,—the close contact between Faculty and Board and the entire frankness and confidence which have ever marked their relations.

The turn of the tide came in 1852. In that year, as the result of a sermon preached by Dr. Prentiss, a meeting was called at the house of Mr. Charles Butler, at which it was resolved to inaugurate a movement for immediate and full endowment. In the course of the next twenty years, through the united efforts of the friends of the Seminary, nearly a million dollars was raised and the financial stability of the Seminary once for all secured.

The second crisis in the Seminary's history was far more serious and called for courage of a higher order. It was the struggle with the General Assembly which began with the veto of Dr. Briggs' transfer to the Edward Robinson Chair in 1891.

It is not my purpose in this hour consecrated to the forward look to revive old memories. The controversy between the Seminary and the Assembly has become a matter of history, and it is not necessary in this presence to tell again what has been retold so often before. Let the dead past bury its dead. Our interest in the struggle to-day is in its revelation of the spirit of the Seminary.

I can remember as if it were yesterday the intensity of feeling which marked those early days. The controversy between the Seminary and the Assembly was at its height during the first years of my official connection with the Seminary Faculty. With what quiet patience all who were concerned carried themselves during this great ordeal, none could know better than the younger men who saw them in the intimacy of the classroom and of the Faculty meeting. The work of the Seminary proceeded as quietly as if nothing were happening without. We used to say, half in jest, and yet I think it was literally true, that the only place where you could go without hearing the Briggs case discussed was Union Seminary. Yet, underneath this quiet exterior a great fire was burning. It was a time that tried men's souls. Old ties were sundered; lifelong friendships severed. Every motive that could be brought to bear upon men was used to influence the Directors and friends of the Seminary to abandon this faithful servant of God whom the highest court of their own church had publicly adjudged a heretic. Financial support was cut off, motives were impugned, students turned aside to other seminaries, but the men at the helm never faltered for an instant. They had taken their course deliberately and under a high sense of responsibilty to God, and they kept it unfalteringly to the end.

For you younger men, sitting in this beautiful chapel today, with every sight and sound about you ministering to the sense of peace and beauty, it is difficult to realize what you owe to those who fought your battles in the past. With a great price they won the liberty to which we were born. I think of Butler and Dana, and Jesup and Dodge and Cuthbert Hall and James and Brown, and all the honored roll of faces whom we miss to-day. Would that they could be with us to rejoice in the new era which their sacrifices and steadfast courage have made possible. Of the living, one name only I will name, our leader through those years of storm and stress, through the providence of God preserved to enjoy in the ripeness of his age the veneration of the sons of Union, our beloved ex-President, Thomas S. Hastings, wise in counsel, courteous in manner, unswerving in courage, trusted leader of men who were themselves accustomed to lead, his name will be held in remembrance wherever men love liberty and honor truth.

A fourth impression which I have carried away from my survey is that of catholicity of spirit. I have said that the founders were New School men, and that means that they were willing to work with anybody who was willing to work with them. From the first the doors of the Seminary have been open to men of all denominations, and all shades of theological opinion have found shelter within its walls. Whatever was of interest to the church of Christ here or across the sea has found a quick response in the hearts of Faculty and students. Nowhere has Christ's prayer that his disciples might all be one been prayed more fervently than within these walls.

To this eager love for unity must be traced the one serious mistake in policy which the annals of the Seminary disclose—I mean the so-called compact of 1870. This was an agreement between the Seminary and the General Assembly, by which the former agreed to grant the Assembly the right of veto over its professors, provided the latter would relinquish, in the case of the seminaries under its control, the right of direct appointment of professors which it had hitherto exercised. This action was taken at the earnest request of Dr. William Adams, the leader of the New School in the reunion movement, and one of the most influential members of the Board. Himself an ardent lover of liberty, chosen by common acclaim as the one American Christian fitted to voice his country's welcome to the Evangelical Alliance at its first meeting on this side of the sea, so great was his zeal for the unity of the church that he was willing that the Seminary, which he loved and served, should surrender some part of her own liberty, if by doing so she could help others to a larger freedom. The decision was not made without searching of heart on the part of the Directors and, in the case of one of them, Mr. D. Willis James, with grave misgivings. Time proved the action mistaken and in due course the Board resumed the power which for the time it had surrendered. But if it was a mistake, it was a mistake that honored those who made it.

The same spirit of catholicity accounts for the last step taken by the Seminary in its progress toward complete freedom, namely, the abolition of the requirement of subscription to the Westminster Confession. This action was taken on November 15, 1904, when Dr. Charles Cuthbert Hall was President of the Faculty. In place of the previous requirement it was provided that each new member of the Board and of the Faculty should in the presence of the Board express his adherence to the principles of the institution as set forth in the Preamble of January 18, 1836, and the Charter of March 27, 1839. Further action provided that the Directors should be members in good and regular standing in some evangelical church, that the professors of Systematic Theology and Pastoral Theology should be ordained ministers of the Gospel, and that all the members of the Faculty should satisfy the Board of their Christian faith and life.

This action must not be understood as a departure from the original principles of the Seminary. On the contrary it was their natural consummation. If subscription was abolished it was not that we wished to believe less, but that we might be free to believe more. Above all, it was that we might open our doors to Christians of every name, that they might enter in and share our work with us. For years this principle had been applied to the student body. Now at last it has been extended to the members of the Faculty and of the Board.

I have said that this action was taken under Dr. Hall's presidency, and with the name I mention one who was himself the very embodiment of the spirit of catholicity. I can see him to-day as he stood in the old library at 700 Park Avenue, when he first met the student body as President-elect, his face radiant with that sunny smile which we came to know so well. I need not remind you how quickly he won his way to the hearts of all whom he touched, or speak of the many improvements which he introduced into the Seminary life. The readjustment of the scholarship system on its present basis, the provisions of the Social Room and of the social spirit, without which the room would have been useless, the baths and the handball courts, the new home for the Union Settlement, the redecoration of the Adams Chapel, and the institution of the new service, the quiet communion seasons at eventide, the kindled enthusiasm for missions,—all of these and more we owe to him whose face we miss to-day.

Much as he did for us, he was more than all that he did, and, as we survey these spacious buildings and study their refined decoration and graceful form, they seem to be the incarnation in stone of that exquisite personality, himself the expression in human life of the spirit of religion pure and undefiled.

Two final impressions, and I am done. One is of the spirit of service, the other of the wealth of personality which the story of Union reveals.

On the first I can touch lightly, not because it is less important, but because it is all important. It is that for which all the rest of which I have spoken exists. If our fathers trusted the truth, it was because they had proved its power in service. If they believed in thorough preparation, it was in order that they might serve better. If they were courageous in conflict, it was because they valued the right to serve so highly that they would suffer no man to rob them of it. If, finally, they were catholic in spirit, it was because they were disciples of him whose kingdom is worldwide and who came to seek and to save the lost.

We have not realized our ideal—far from it—but at least we can say that we have never appreciated our ideal more clearly or cherished it more whole-heartedly than we do today. If we have established ourselves on these heights, close by the great university whose throbbing life we can feel pulsing through our own veins, it is not that we would abandon the city to its need, but that we may gain added knowledge to aid us in the solution of its problems. The Settlement on East One Hundred and Fourth Street, with its spacious play-ground, surrounded by crowded tenements, is as truly a part of the Seminary as this stately pile on Morningside Heights, and far away on the frontiers of the distant West, or in the lumber camps of Maine, or among the Negroes of the Southland, or in China and Japan and India and the islands of the sea, wherever a son of Union in the spirit of his Master is grappling hand to hand with the problems of human misery and human ignorance, there the spirit of Union is present and the heart of the Seminary finds expression.

The other impression is of the wealth of personality. To no other institution on God's earth, I verily believe, has it been given in a similar space of time to gather so large a cluster of devoted friends. What a roll it is that passes before the mind as imagination recalls those who have gone before. Clergymen like Absalom Peters, Erskine Mason, Albert Barnes, Samuel Hanson Cox, George L. Prentiss, Edwin F. Hatfield, Henry B. Smith, Edward Robinson, William Adams, William G. T. Shedd, Philip Schaff, Roswell D. Hitchcock, and Charles Cuthbert Hall. Laymen like Knowles Taylor, Richard T. Haines, William M. Halstead, Norman White, Anson Phelps, Fisher Howe, Frederick Marquand, James Brown, Edwin D. Morgan, Charles Butler, D. Hunter McAlpin, William E. Dodge, Morris K. Jesup, and last but not least that far-sighted merchant and simple follower of Jesus Christ, whose name this chapel commemorates. Others in this company will speak his praises in words more eloquent than mine, but I cannot deny myself my tribute to his memory. For more than forty years a Director of Union Theological Seminary, for ten years its Vice-President, always its generous benefactor and wise counselor, he was its faithful friend in adversity as in prosperity, and his final gift was but the crown of a life which was full of giving.

One other there is, of whom piety will not suffer me to be silent, though piety makes it difficult for me to speak. We miss to-day one face that was with us at the laying of the corner-stone a year ago. It is a face that has grown familiar to many generations of Union Seminary students, not only through his official position as President of the Seminary, but in the more informal intercourse of the home. Bound to the Seminary by ancestral ties, for forty years identified with its interests as Director, Vice-President and President, intimately associated with the smallest details of its affairs, it was to him that Mr. James first communicated his generous purpose, and it was to him that he confided the execution of his trust. It was not his privilege to see the completion of these buildings, into whose every stone he had built his thought and love, but to the end he carried them on his heart. They were the last responsibility which he laid down, and the last continued conversation which I had with him only a week before his death had to do with them.

What was the secret of this devotion? What spell does Union possess which can bind to her service men such as these whose names we have mentioned? Let us find our answer in the words spoken by our late President at his last public appearance with us, when he laid the corner-stone of the new buildings:

"As the representative of the Board of Directors," so the

solemn words run, "I have been requested to lay the corner-stone of this group of buildings, the future home of the Union Theological Seminary, an institution founded in 1836 by godly men 'to prepare young men for the service of Christ in the work of the ministry.' Sharing with the Founders the belief that for all enduring religious work 'other foundation can no man lay than that is laid, which is Jesus Christ,' the Directors set apart this stone as the symbol of the spiritual foundation upon which this Seminary rests."

Six and twenty years ago the friends of Union Seminary met upon another hilltop to dedicate a new home. How little they anticipated what the next quarter of a century would bring forth. "The present location," said Dr. Hitchcock, in his memorable dedicatory address, "is apparently for many decades, if not for all time. This commanding site, so near the centre of the island, is in little danger of losing its advantages. Right behind us is the great Central Park, close around us are hospitals, schools and galleries of art, trophies and adornments of an advancing civilization, but this institution of sacred learning which we dedicate to-day, interpreter of God's word, herald of God's grace, outranks them all."

Only yesterday I stood on the old site, now a heap of ruins, and as I recalled the words which I have just quoted in your hearing, these other words, spoken by an older member of the Seminary many years before, rose unbidden to my lips: "Nothing, my brethren, is great in this world but the Kingdom of Jesus Christ. Nothing but that to a spiritual eye has the air of permanency."

Nothing in this world is great but the Kingdom of Jesus Christ, nothing else is permanent. Brick and mortar may decay, stones may crumble into dust, one generation of workers after another may pass away, the Kingdom of Jesus Christ endures forever. This is the ground of our confidence as we look forward to the new and splendid future that we face. These noble buildings, massive as they are, are to us but the symbol of a reality far more enduring, even the Kingdom of our Lord and Saviour, Jesus Christ, God manifest in man, the same yesterday, to-day and forever.

2.

Some Elements of Religious Progress

Address by President Jacob Gould Schurman, Sc.D., LL.D.

After the very scholarly and instructive and inspiring address of Dr. Brown, to which you have listened, I need offer no apology for saying, that the thing about Union Theological Seminary which most impresses an outsider, like myself, among all the characteristic things which he has mentioned is its catholicity. When your President honored me with an invitation to speak on this occasion, he didn't limit me inexorably to thirty minutes, but as he understood that I was very busy, he diplomatically remarked that it was not necessary to speak more than thirty or forty minutes. I think I can not do better than attempt to describe as I see them, and as I have tried to give them expression in my own mind, some of the phases of religious progress which our generation has witnessed.

It seemed to me, as I have said, the Union Theological Seminary was the embodiment of that spirit. And when I thought of the scholars who have been and are of its Faculty, the names of many of whom you have heard this evening, I felt that it in no inconsiderable measure had contributed to this religious progress in America. Nevertheless, I recognize that the movement is larger than any institution, and therefore it seemed to me that in a sense it might be said that Union Theological Seminary was the effect of that spirit. And a notable institution this Seminary is, notable, and as it seems to me unique.

Free and unfettered it devotes itself to the pursuit of truth in the whole realm of theological science and at the same time it trains young men to the noble calling of the Christian ministry. As it devotes itself to effort in this field it is akin with the university, and I appeal to this kindred spirit for sympathy and tolerance. To that spirit I appeal as I endeavor to describe some of the phases of progress of which we have been conscious in the religious sphere in the last thirty or forty years.

In the first place, and to put it strongly, I think we have witnessed a shifting of emphasis from individualism to the improvement or amelioration of the condition of society. I am not saying that this change is altogether good. I can easily see or imagine in certain cases that it is carried too far, and that men are thinking of the improvement of society who ought to be thinking about their own souls and characters and about Jesus Christ.

Nevertheless it is a change which has come over the religious world. I think there has never been a time since Christianity came into the world that there is so much sympathy for the poor and concern for the condition of the poor than there is to-day in all ranks of society and especially in the Christian Church, and when we recall that the Founder of this Church was especially solicitous about the condition of the poor, we can at least find no fault with this shifting of emphasis in the attitude and work of the modern church. I think, however, it becomes us to remember that our attitude is not and cannot be the same as that of two thousand years ago. Knowledge and exact science have made great progress not only in the last two thousand years but in the last two hundred years, and if the early church thought of relieving suffering, the church of to-day, certainly, with the scientific atmosphere through which it lives and moves, will more and more think of the prevention of suffering, and as there can be no effective prevention of any evil, whether in the individual's life or in the life of society without the knowledge of causes, we shall come more and more to studying the causes of social evil and of the suffering and ills of society. It may well be that some of the subjects which that worthy of 1837 desired to see incorporated in the curriculum of this institution, Hebraic, Greek, Chaldean, Syriac and Arabic, will in the course of time be omitted and your students will pay more attention to useful sciences, with reference both to the normal condition of society and the evils and sufferings of society. I say this, because I know at the present time that when ministers and especially young ministers, who are devoted to the welfare of their fellowmen, and burning with desire to do them good, face this great social problem of our time they very easily swing to socialism, as though socialism were the only scheme that offered relief for the toiling masses. I am inclined to think that when we know more than we generally know to-day about the causes of social evils, we shall take up with less ambitious schemes and try for reform and improvement here a little and there a little.

For instance: justice is the fundamental foundation of

the State. Plato says of the ideal commonwealth which he calls his republic, that it is merely justice enlarged. All of us, in the church and out of the church, have a right to insist that justice shall be done in the modern State, and if, for instance, we find the burdens of taxation falling more heavily on the poor than they fall on the rich and the well-to-do, then, in the name of justice we have a right to demand that these systems of indirect taxation which produce such an effect shall be modified, and that some device—income tax or what not—shall be found which shall compel the prosperous classes of the community to support the government in proportion to their means and to the relief of the great mass of the poor and indigent.

But to continue. The Christian Church is devoted to peace on earth and good will to men. It is the shame of Christendom, the burning, intolerable shame of Christendom, that so large a proportion of all the wealth produced in our industrial communities is used to provide the instrumentalities of warfare. Socialism does well to cry out against the militant spirit of our time and denounce it. I believe that if all branches of the Christian Church in all countries denounce it with the same fervor and earnestness that statesmen of the great powers of the world would find a solution of this problem or give up their jobs.

A second change which I notice in the religious world is a reaction from dogmatic religion and a recoil towards what I shall call spiritual religion. All the religions of the world, as I understand them, have three elements. They have an intellectual element; they must, therefore, be dogmatic. They have an æsthetic element, and, therefore, have rituals, and they have a moral and a spiritual element. For hundreds, I might almost say, for thousands of years, the Christian religion has laid stress on dogma as the essential feature of religion. The earliest religions laid stress on ritual. A man among those communities would not be a heretic or a wrong believer, but he would be a wrongdoer because he did not perform the rituals in the right way.

But we are coming, nowadays, to feel, I think, throughout the religious world in general that neither of these elements is the essential element in religion, though both of them will, I suppose, always be present in all religions. We are coming to realize more and more that the essence of religion is the spirit and attitude and freedom of mind with which they approach their problems.

The Founder of the Christian religion paid no attention to ritual or to creed. He passed them sublimely by, and the thing I am trying to describe perhaps I can express best if I should say that we seem to me to be rediscovering, after nearly two thousand years, Jesus Christ and his religion. There are reasons, no doubt, which have hastened this movement, appearing outside the Christian Church itself. The most potent of these has been the development of exact science. It is simply impossible for us nowadays to take up the same attitude toward dogmas which was assumed towards them thirty, forty or fifty years ago. I do not mean that we are bound to accept the speculations and hypotheses of rash inquirers, who call themselves physical scientists or historical critics, but I do mean that both scientists and historians have built up, in the course of the last two or three generations, and notably in the last fifty years, a body of exact and verified science, and this science has become in its general phases the commonplace of popular thought, and the methods of research which these investigators have followed are the only methods in which we now have confidence. These things have been assimilated by the people, and are now an expression of the spirit of the times. They have all been verified and interest us all, and consequently, whether we would or not, we simply find it impossible to take the attitude towards dogmas which the human race possessed prior to the advent of this scientific knowledge and these scientific methods.

A generation ago our teachers and theological schools were full of the warfare between science and religion, but better methods have reconciled that warfare. Professorships were founded in our institutions of learning for that purpose. I think I may say that to-day this conflict is over. The age of the world, the origin of the earth, the manner of its development, the succession of living organisms on its surface, the evolution of man, the history of the Jews, the evidence of miracles; these are questions which do not to-day enter into the religion of educated or thoughtful men; that religion is something, as it seems to me, deeper and more divine.

It is not whether the mere logical minds and intellects can grasp and correctly formulate certain mysterious propositions ranging over the whole field of metaphysics, a large portion of the field of natural science and a not inconsiderable part of the field of history of the human race, but whether the will and the conscience are attuned to the spirit of Jesus Christ.

The third change which I notice in this period which I am

surveying I may describe as the development of the Christian Church away from sectarianism and towards the spirit of world religion. A generation ago or certainly two generations ago groups of men took sides on these questions, which, as I have said, are for us fading into unimportance, and the whole Christian Church was split up into sects and co-operation between them was almost impossible, and a spirit often very different from a spirit of brotherly love prevailed amongst them. That seems to me to be disappearing. The different branches of the church are coming together. They can co-operate in the common educational, philanthropic and often missionary undertakings. I do not mean that differences of religious belief are destined to disappear. Nations differ and individuals differ and beliefs are an expression of national and personal character, and we may therefore fairly assume that differences will continue. My point is that these differences do not appear as large as they did, or do not raise up between us the walls or partitions they did, but that in spite of them we believe the things we have in common are infinitely more important than the things in which we differ. The things in which we differ may be not only of personal or national character or as to historical circumstances, but as we understand the reason for these differences they thus become less important in our eyes. But that is not all that I mean by this third change I am endeavoring to describe. It is not merely that we are growing big, but we are taking our religion to all quarters of the globe and we are working harmoniously in those missionary fields. Oh, more than that, we are coming to appreciate what is good in the religions of foreign nations and foreign races. Three weeks ago I invited to preach at Cornell University the Rev. Dr. Harada, Japanese Christian and Professor of the University at Kyoto. It was one of the most instructive and interesting discourses I have ever heard. His subject was "The National Characteristics of the Japanese, considered as Helps and Hindrances to the Acceptance of the Christian Religion." He said that the great mission of the Christian religion in his country is to bring into life the highest ideals, and he said, "If you conceive of Christianity as the religion of self-sacrifice, then if the cross was a stumbling block to the Jews and foolishness to the Greeks, it appealed to what was deepest and noblest in the minds and hearts of the Japanese." "The mission," he said, "the great mission of the Christian Church in my country is to quicken into life ideals we already possess." He did not mean to say that it would do nothing else for the Japanese, but on the contrary he said to those who have any knowledge of the personality of the Japanese that he felt it might be the mission of the Christian religion to develop a deeper sense of personality, personality of God and personality of man and thus arouse in them a deepening sense of personality and growing sense also of human responsibility. I think a generation or two ago it would have been almost impossible for Christian people to sympathize with what we may call unity in Christian missions, as described by Dr. Brown, and as shown here to-day.

May I go further? I think I see a still further line of development. The Christian religion, we believe, is the noblest of all religions. It is the only religion that can become a world religion, but my belief is, and it is founded on some observation and experience, that it is just in proportion as we carry that religion to foreign nations and they assimilate it that we ourselves get a new insight into it. In other words, we shall not know what the perfect Christian religion is until the nations of the world have heard it and assimilated it, and the perfect Christian religion will be what is revealed by this universal religious life of mankind in that distant day, or perhaps not distant day when they all come to enjoy its blessings.

Finally, and not disconnected with what I have already said, I think we are laying more and more stress on the religion which Christ taught and of which his own life was the living precept and embodiment. He did not perplex men's minds with difficult intellectual problems; he challenged their laws; he appealed to their conscience; he talked of right and duty, of love, of devotion, of self-sacrifice; these are the hard things demanded of us, but I think more and more as the years go by the Christian Church is coming to recognize that these are the essential things in religion,—the Christ-like spirit, the Christ-like life; and wherever we find these things, whether in the churches or out of the churches, whether in Christian lands or in so-called heathen lands, we shall say, "There is the spirit of Christ." Remember what he himself said, "Other sheep I have which are not of this fold."

These are a few of the changes which I have felt it proper to call to your attention at this time in connection with this great celebration. I chose this subject, because as I said in my own mind the Union Theological Seminary stands so pre-eminently for this kind of work, and as Dr. William Adams Brown has already said, "The Seminary stands not only for scholarship, not only for intellectual life, not only for catholicity of spirit but for a practical devotion to the service of mankind." I like that note; I like that combination; that rounds up all the supreme things of man's life.

My wish for Union Seminary and for its members now and their successive generations is that on the one hand they may retain the intellectual freedom which they have and have so conspicuously shown, retain it as it is retained by scientists and philosophers, but on the other hand that they combine with it as they have already combined in the past the devotion which characterizes the martyr and the saint. It is absolutely essential that these two things be combined in the life of individuals and institutions if their work is to be made permanent, as the great danger of all living institutions and of all living movements is in the lack of earnestness. We cannot have listened to the address of Dr. Brown without feeling that thus far this institution has happily escaped that danger.

The one thing needful is that men shall become better. This however is an individual concern. Consequently it is through the reform and improvement of indivduals that the religion of Christ is to make its way in the world. Not only is the progress of the Christian religion effected by individuals, but the essential work of that religion is in the mind and soul of the individual. Of course this is not to disparage philanthropic enterprises for improving the sanitation, the housing, or other environmental conditions of the poor. And indeed we must recognize that until the primal physical necessities are reasonably satisfied it is almost useless to try to improve the moral and intellectual conditions of the individuals who compose the mass. Furthermore, it may be asserted that it is the duty of all Christians to make the environment and external conditions of the poor more favorable than they are today. But when all this is said and when all allowance is made for other qualifying conditions, the fundamental fact remains that the Founder of the Christian religion appealed to the heart and conscience of the individual man. And any interpretation of the Christian religion which ignores this all-essential function gives us the body without the soul of that religion.

VI

THE ADDRESSES AT THE ALUMNI MEETING

1 The Seminary's New Era, by the Reverend President Francis Brown, D.D., LL.D.

2 The Claim of the Kingdom upon the Seminary, by the Reverend Henry H. Stebbins, D.D.

3 Our Gospel, by the Reverend William P. Merrill, D.D.

4 The Christian Missionary and his Message in the Twentieth Century, by the Reverend President Howard S. Bliss, D.D.

I.

The Seminary's New Era

By the Reverend President Francis Brown, D.D., LL.D.

Mr. President and Members of the Alumni Association:

You will all agree with me that a new era it is. We are introduced to a new period in the Seminary's life. It is not the first step in the introduction that we are taking to-day. If the Seminary had faltered when the attack came twenty years ago there could have been no new era. If free and reverent scholarship had been discouraged there would have been none. If that "extreme of ecclesiastical domination" against which our founders spoke had been permitted twenty years ago, there would have been none. If there had been no enfranchisement by new terms of subscription the new era would have halted and lagged. The great things were done by the insight and courage of the men just back of us, men whom we know, men of whom some are alive still. The new era was born in steadfast bravery and spiritual vision. This site, and these buildings are splendid, and their worth is doubled by the fact that they are due, primarily, to those who already had expressed their vision in noble testimony, and fought the fight with courage. But these buildings launch us upon a new era not because they are more significant than the intellectual and spiritual forces which have been working, but because they give these forces a new opportunity. The essential forces are primary. The new equipment gives them free course. Because of both, it is, indeed, a new era that we are facing. And what do we see?

1. We see a great horizon. It is hard to set limits to it. I pity the man, who, in such a case, does not reach out, strongly, into the unknown. It is an era for the imagination. Great pictures of the future take shape. Plans almost form themselves without straining of the mind. The possibilities are bewildering. But we are not looking with flickering, feeble gaze. We see what may be as a sculptor sees his statue in the block, and as the architect sees the cathedral be-

fore stone is laid upon stone. It may not be realized quite as we see it, but we, all of us, are stirred by the outlook toward the shaping of an instrument great and good, for the world-wide service of God. These plans do not stir our pride; their magnificence has something awful in it, which sends us to our knees. Are our material resources adequate to their fulfillment? Hardly, yet. Is our physical strength sufficient? Doubtless, as long as God needs us—and then the next relay of men will come on. Is our mental power healthful and competent? We have not already attained but we follow after, if that we may apprehend. Is our personal influence and moral sensitiveness and spiritual energy ample stock for our great business? These are questions that we ask ourselves. And we are giving no self-confident or jaunty answers. We know that we can do nothing, as we ought to do it, without God.

2. It must be therefore an era of faith. We cannot go into it without belief in the realities—in the reality of God, in the revelation through Jesus Christ, in the forgiveness of sins, in a supreme power for setting wrong things right—to the last stubbornness of heart, the lowest depth of infamy, the very end of the world—in the real triumph of righteousness. We need faith in our opportunity—no prostrating fear of it—expectancy, in every aspect of it, because God gives it to us. We need faith in the message of Jesus, which is our gospel; in the worth of his character, and the essential necessity of his salvation;—in the conquest of self, and the reproduction of his life, in its simplest elements, under the greatest variety of conditions and circumstances,—in the possibilities germinating in ourselves and our neighbours, which hold the promise of a redeemed world, and make it both desirable and certain that human life shall at length be filled with the divine, and controlled by it.

3. It must be an era of efficiency. Dreamers may still have their part to play, but it must be to inspire the doers. Idle dreams are ignoble. It is the patient, faithful, efficient doers of the work that justify bold dreams. We must train men to master the technique of their art. It cannot be done by simply applying high pressure to the spiritual life. Patient, quiet, steadfast work, in study and practice, is the channel of expression for real spiritual life, and no mean one, when it signifies knowing your business. You want men who can do things, and we want to produce them, but the process cannot be hurried, and it takes concentration of purpose and long,

hard work. The reason why some ministers are inefficient is that many ministers have too low a conception of efficiency, and know too little how efficiency can be attained. You, who know, will not blame us for trying to make our training mentally severe. It is the condition of efficiency.

No doubt some things are more important than others. We are constantly revising our judgment of values, and acting accordingly. I should like to set before you, if there were time, our present view of a curriculum in theology, under the three rubrics of the essential gospel, the situation in the world which needs the gospel, and the means by which the gospel may be brought home to the world. Think these subjects through and see if your thought of training for the ministry does not gain unity and insistence. This great establishment must be put to the largest and most intelligent use for the Kingdom of God. We ask you to encourage us in making our new era an era of efficiency.

4. It is an era of fellowship. We want fellowship with all Christians, and with all earnest people who are not Christians, in their work for righteousness, as far as they will let us have it. "He that is not against us is on our part." Our business is too high for rivalry. We seek fellowship and sympathy on all hands, and especially with all with whom Christ holds fellowship, or would have, if they would permit it. We have no hostilities or bitternesses or grudges to cherish—as far as we understand ourselves. We may have prejudices but we hope they are like "that salutary prejudice known as love of country"—salutary prejudices known as love of the Seminary, and what we think to be the truth, and love of liberty, and love of Jesus Christ, and desire to be like him, and to see a world of people like him. If we have meaner prejudices we are not proud of them. This is the kind we wish to have. But these do not destroy our sense of fellowship—in which small party names and sectarian distinctions are merged and lost—it gives our fellowship value and fulness.

Your fellowship, who have now come here, must be with each other, and with us whose duty is here, and our fellowship must be with each other and with you. We can do great things by helping each other and holding together. But true fellowship is not at all content with the like-minded and congenial. Christianity is weighed twenty times a day against other religions, old and new. We shall honor them all for whatever they do to lift men towards righteousness and God.

And if anyone of them proclaims as its essence the obligation of each man to share the richness of his life and not to hoard it, and lives this out in the simple strength of God, by the practice of men's days, busy and hard beset, it is Christ's religion, under another name, in its unalloyed product. The only advantage that Christianity then has lies in a broader and deeper practice of fellowship with God and man, giving oneself loyally to them both, as Jesus Christ did and does forevermore. We shall never be afraid of any religion's seeming too much like that of Christ when we are once convinced that the world of people will have entered the divine fellowship, with knowledge, heart and purpose all together—when every religion is made entirely Christian, after Christ's manner, and the world has grown a brotherhood, in rich exchange of the earthly gifts and treasures of the soul—to the glory of God, the Father.

The Seminary lives in its alumni. It is strengthened, more than you know, by your presence here, and your generous loyalty. If *you* were not full of large plans for God, and great faith, and efficiency, and the spirit of fellowship, the Seminary would be an empty name. Help us, brothers, to make it *more* than an empty name. Help us, by your own ardent service of Christ and his kingdom, to realize the possibilities of the new era—to train new generations even better than you were trained, to bear testimony to the heroic life, to take our share in the divine conquest of the world.

2.

The Claim of the Kingdom upon the Seminary

By the Reverend Henry H. Stebbins, D.D.

Mr. President of the Alumni, Mr. President of the Faculty, undergraduate students and fellow Alumni of this dear Seminary that is exciting so many delightful and hallowed memories and that is inspiring so many Alumni to unprecedented hopes:

The claim of the Kingdom upon the Seminary is, as I at least conceive it, that the Seminary should interpret the Kingdom of God as revealed in the Old and New Testaments of the Word of God and should train all applicants for the service of the King.

To such end the Kingdom would venture to submit the four cardinal points of a compass, as it were, whereby the Seminary may steer her course to the desired heaven.

1. The first cardinal point is the Seminary herself.

The Kingdom recognizes the Seminary as the institution, above all others, that should unfold the Kingdom in all its bearings, whether the Kingdom that cometh within, the Kingdom that cometh not with observation, or the Kingdom visible.

The Kingdom reminds us that, humanly speaking, the Seminary is the supreme resource of the Church; that the Church looks to the Seminary to turn out ministers thoroughly furnished to go into all the world, near or distant, and to preach the Gospel of the Kingdom to every creature.

The Kingdom claims that the Seminary should be the repository of all possible information about the Kingdom, information concerning its nature, its scope, its subjects, its present day demands, its prospects and its consummation in heart and life, in the individual, in society, in the state, in the world, to the end that God's Kingdom may fully come in the doing of his will on earth as it is done in heaven.

Further, the Kingdom claims that the teaching force of the Seminary should be second to none, either as to acquisition or ability to impart, and in popular fashion a force that should teach with authority and not as the scribes.

The Kingdom claims that the Seminary should blaze the way, should take the initiative, should, under the impulse of a faith that is the substance of things hoped for, the evidence of things not seen, anticipate the demand as commerce anticipates the market, so that as the servants of the King go about their appointed work, they may stab wide awake the social consciousness and the social conscience of those with whom they have to do, thereby attracting in growing numbers those who shall spend and be spent in the active, practical propagation of the Kingdom of Heaven on earth, who shall discern readily any given environment, who shall be instant in season, out of season, in knowing what is to be done and how to do it most feasibly and permanently, and who, in a word, shall incite to a militant altruism in the service of the King.

2. The second cardinal point in the proposed compass is the federated church.

While the Kingdom would have the Seminary recognize herself as, providentially, the first of institutions for meeting the demands of the Kingdom, it would have her recognize the Church as the supreme instrumentality, humanly speaking, for the promotion of the Kingdom, not, however, by any means, to the exclusion of other agencies, but to their distinct subordination.

There is vital reason, the Kingdom contends, for the preaching of the gospel of the Kingdom, the preaching, backed by the authority of "Thus saith the Lord."

The Kingdom claims that it springs directly from the bosom of religion, in distinction from mere philanthropy or humanitarianism; that it inculcates, first of all, the most comprehensive love to God, and along with that and separable from it, love to man, and that the Church is the obvious means to that end.

The Kingdom sees the Church as the exponent of the Christianity of Christ, as His divinely designed successor, and that accordingly she is true to the fullness of her mission only as she looks at the world as Jesus looked at it and stands, in relation to men, as Jesus did, and ministers as Jesus did to the manifold ills and limitations of human life.

And the Kingdom appeals to the New Testament, to say nothing of the Old Testament, which abounds in teaching and injunction about the Kingdom, for overwhelming evidence in corroboration of its claim as to the primacy of the Church as the instrumentality for the diffusion of the laws of the Kingdom, in their manifold application to the individual and to society.

In this connection the Kingdom congratulates the Church upon the following resolution adopted by the Presbytery of New York:

"RESOLVED, that we recognize the gospel of Christ as the supreme remedy for every form of evil, and the church of Christ as the agency by which the world is to be regenerated and saved, and, therefore, we believe that the moral teachings of Christ must be applied to every sphere of life, and that the church should bear her testimony for righteousness and purity in all human affairs."

So with renewed assurance the Kingdom maintains that the Church needs to be exploited, that she needs to come to her own, needs to be stimulated to make her calling and election sure in the world realm of social service; that she needs to be socialized, and to become a radiating social center, exemplifying brotherly love, a love aiming to fulfill every jot and every tittle of the laws of service and sacrifice.

And it is the Church as such which the Kingdom has in view, the church in the country, as well as in the City, the church in foreign parts as well as in the homeland.

Indeed, the Kingdom points with pride to the vastly broadened scope of missions. At first, as we are reminded, the missionary's equipment, aside from a consecrated heart, consisted of a Bible and a sun hat, or, as a little girl is reported to have conceived it: A man standing under a tree and reading the Bible to everybody who passed by.

Witness now, is the challenge of the Kingdom, witness now, by contrast, the school, the college, all that is comprehended under medical missions, and all that is signified by industrial missions, to say nothing of the wonders of the printing press and the fruits of Christian Sociology.

The Kingdom points to the following list of things with which a missionary is about to sail to Africa: A turbine wheel, a saw-mill with planer and jointer, mortising machine, etc., a traction or motor engine and gang plow, a reaper and binder, a thresher, two horse seed drills, appliances for a school of agriculture, school supplies and a hospital outfit.

Moreover, and in the same connection, the Kingdom reminds us that to the peoples who on earth do dwell there were never so many open doors as to-day. Indeed, missionaries report that doors have been taken from their hinges. Not from Macedonia alone, but from every quarter, the cry is heard, "Come over and help us," which cry, being interpreted, is a cry for the blessings of the Kingdom of Heaven in the interest of which Jesus Christ came to the Kingdom of Earth.

Still further, never have the peoples of the earth been so well understood as they are to-day, and never so responsive.

Such is the plea of the Kingdom, and the Kingdom submits that the citizens of the Kingdom are bound to hear and heed that cry or they are recreant to the will of their King.

The Kingdom, while making careful and grateful record of the fact that the supporters, by word and deed, of social service are to a great extent connected with the Church, and while delighting in the institutional church, as a progressive approach to the desired goal, yet urges the Church to identify herself more prominently and intimately with the many-sided service of the Kingdom, and to embosom it in her working creed that she is the pre-eminent means for the promulgation and expansion of the Kingdom of Heaven on earth.

The Kingdom would emphasize the Church of it in distinction from the churches. For the Kingdom does not recognize churches, it recognizes but one Church, the holy Catholic Church. Consequently the Kingdom stands for the speediest possible federation or unification, organic or spiritual, or combination, call it what we will, of all the churches of God, only, pleads the Kingdom, let it be in fulfillment of Jesus' prayer of intercession:

" That they all may be one; as thou, Father, are in me, and I in thee, that they also may be one in us: that the world may believe that thou hast sent me."

And, inasmuch as citizenship in the Kingdom is more inclusive than membership in the Church, the Kingdom would have the Seminary take into account, in this connection, all who, in the Church or outside the Church, are cultivating pure and undefiled religion, all who aim to fulfill God's requirement to do justly, to love mercy, and to walk humbly with their God, all who are living righteously, soberly and godly in this present evil world, and who would join the forces of those disposed to labor for the universal prevalence of whatsoever things are true and honest and just and pure and lovely and of good report.

3. The third cardinal point in the proposed compass is the Bible.

The Kingdom insists that the Book of books in the curriculum of the Seminary, so far as such curriculum has to do with the Kingdom, should be the Bible, the English Bible, and that it should be handled in such masterful fashion as to make it quick and powerful, sharper than any two-edged sword.

The Kingdom holds that there is no consistent theory or application of the Kingdom apart from the Bible, and that the worthiest treatises on the Kingdom have been consciously or unconsciously, the echo of what the Bible declares and illustrates.

The Kingdom affirms that there is no phase of itself, that there is no social law worth while and no line of social service, whether having to do with the child or the adult, with body or mind or heart, with the family or the city or the state, or with industrial life or with politics, or education, or crime, or with defective and dependent life, or outcasts, or with hospitals or any of the institutions of philanthropy or with settlements, that is not anticipated and fundamentally provided for by the glorious Gospel of the blessed God.

And the Kingdom imposes upon the Seminary the task of coupling with every department of social service, the law,

BROADWAY AT 120TH STREET

or the principle, or the precept, or the sentiment contained in the book of final authority.

4. The fourth cardinal point of the compass the Kingdom would command to the Seminary is the Christ.

The Kingdom would have the Seminary, in its relation to social service, exalt the personality of Jesus Christ. It would have the Seminary hail Him as King and give Him the glory due unto His name.

The Kingdom would have the Seminary discriminate between the King and the Kingdom, as between Christ and Christianity, so keeping the personal life more than the impersonal instrumentality, before the reverent eye and the grateful, loyal and affectionate heart of every citizen of the Kingdom.

The Kingdom would have the Seminary behold in Christ the Teacher come from God, the chief among the ten thousand who throughout the ages, have thought or spoken or written upon the problematic, yet fascinating theme of the Kingdom. It would have the sociology taught at the Seminary not merely Christianized, but shot through and through with the personality of Jesus Christ.

Honor to whom honor is due, pleads the Kingdom. Let the name of Jesus stand above every name, as the prince of authorities on the subject so vital and of such world-wide significance.

The Kingdom recalls the following sentiment from Professor Peabody of Cambridge:

" In a great orchestra, with all its varied ways of musical expression, there is one person who performs on no instrument whatever, but in whom, none the less, the whole control of harmony and rythm resides.

" Until the leader comes the discordant sounds go their various ways; but at his sign the tuning of the instruments ceases and the symphony begins.

" So it is with spiritual leadership of Jesus Christ. Among the conflicting activities of the present time, His power is not that of one more active among the rest, but that of wisdom, personality, idealism.

" Into the midst of the discordant efforts of men He comes as one having authority; the self-assertion of each instrument of social service is hushed as He gives His sign; and in the surrender of each life to Him, it finds its place in the symphony of all."

The Kingdom would have the Seminary widen its doors

and keep them wide open day and night for all classes and grades of workers, for candidates for the ministry in the technical sense, for church officials, for Sunday school teachers, for members of Men's Guilds and Brotherhoods, of Missionary Societies, of the Young People's Society, of Christian Endeavor, and of the Young Men's Christian Association; for members of the church, for non-ecclesiastical Christians,—for the "children of the unwritten gospel," as Dr. Matheson calls them, for college graduates, for philanthropists of wealth, for merchant princes, in a word, for any and all who would be fitted for the most effective social service in the name of Him who came not to be ministered unto but to minister.

Of course such a policy would make the Seminary coeducational. And there should be shorter as well as longer courses. Just as at Cornell University there are courses of twelve weeks in poultry-raising, horticulture, dairying and general agriculture, so the Seminary should afford brief courses of study, according to the wishes or the necessities of the students.

The Seminary should provide a wide range of electives, or homogeneous groups of subjects in line with the foremost demands of the times; she should provide for night classes and for a summer course; she should require, not leave it optional, of every student, a course in Christian sociology and should permeate with such course the whole period of study from start to finish.

In short, the Seminary should be perennially open for all seeking instruction under its guidance, and should be manned, yes and womaned, if need be (and the Kingdom anticipates that there will be the need), so that the burden of instruction would not be heavier than could be borne consistently. Such is the insistence of the Kingdom.

"A new departure, all this," the Kingdom anticipates the Seminary as exclaiming. "Yes," replies the Kingdom, "yet it is but one of numerous new departures necessitated by the exacting law of adjustment to existing or prospective conditions."

The Kingdom is swift to assure the Seminary that the proposed enlargement of her sphere does not involve the surrender or the curtailment of her present curriculum.

The Kingdom is grateful for the apparent fact that in a considerable percentage of the Seminaries of the United States provision is made for more or less, less rather than more, it would seem, of training along social service lines, thus facing, measurably at least, the responsibility that is upon them and welcoming with diminishing timidity the opportunity to meet such responsibility.

And, again, the Kingdom, while impatient of delay, would concede the necessity of patience and a judicious conservatism. At the same time the Kingdom would spur the Seminary to quicken its pace because of the larger, clearer vision the Church is gaining of the Kingdom, as shown by her parish houses, her institutes, her missions, her settlements, and in general by the institutional character she is making for men of God, men who, as pastors, will take into account the whole man and not merely the soul, who will aim to win to Christ not the individual only, but society as well, and who, in a word, will help to extend the Kingdom in all its length and breadth and height and depth.

My fancy pictures a Seminary modeled after the Gospel plan: a Seminary obedient to the heavenly vision of her obligation and her corresponding opportunity; a Seminary steering her course of conquest according to the compass whose four cardinal points are: the Seminary herself as the institution above all others for the training of competent workers; the federated Church as the instrumentality above every other for the world-wide proclamation and extension of the Kingdom; the Bible as the basic authority of all teaching with reference to the Kingdom, and the Christ as the basic personality of the Kingdom, King of Kings and Lord of Lords, worthy to receive power and riches and wisdom and strength and honor and glory and blessing; a Seminary undenominational, a Seminary with twelve gates, on the east three gates, on the north three gates, on the south three gates and on the west three gates; a Seminary dedicated to the training of all who would preach, practice and propagate the gospel of the Kingdom in the name of Him who came to seek and to save that which was lost; a Seminary that should be the chief repository of the history, the literature, and all current facts respecting the Kingdom; a Seminary so munificently endowed that the administrators of her affairs would take no anxious thought as to ways and means; a Seminary that should be the pride, the joy, the inspiration of the Church which Jesus Christ loved and for which he gave himself, that he might present it unto himself a glorious Church, not having spot or wrinkle or any such thing, but that it should be holy and without blemish; and lastly, a Seminary which should no more be called a Theological Seminary, but a Theological University.

However wide the chasm between fancy and fact in relation to the Seminary, may be to-day, I confess that, as I go round about this ally and resource of our beloved Zion, that as I tell the graceful and symbolic towers thereof, the towers that are and the towers that are to be; that as I mark well her bulwarks of tradition, of affectionate and enriching personality both in professor and in student, and of her world-wide and ineffaceable influence; and that as I consider her palaces of equipment in contrast to what used to be; I see the chasm between fancy and fact bridged by this institution whose new buildings we dedicate on these days of grace, the twenty-seventh, the twenty-eight and the twenty-ninth days of November, in this year of our Lord one thousand nine hundred and ten.

Who knoweth whether the Union Theological Seminary is come to the Kingdom for such a time as this?

So let it be, so far as it is according to the will of Him who taught us, when we pray, to say: " Thy Kingdom come."

3.

Our Gospel

By the Reverend William P. Merrill, D.D.

MR. PRESIDENT AND BROTHERS OF THE ALUMNI:

In presenting this theme I am not thinking so much of the Seminary and the place it should take as of us who are Alumni of the Seminary and the place we should take and the Gospel that we should preach as representatives of that Christian thought and love for which this Seminary stands.

The word " our " is intended to include all those in the ministry of the church, teachers or preachers, who frankly adopt the modern point of view in religion. One of the main characteristics, perhaps the chief distinction of this Seminary, in whose stately new home we rejoice to-day, is that with few exceptions, her graduates are men who welcome reconstruction in religion. Most of us are grateful to our Seminary most of all for breaking for us the shell of tradition, and letting us into life. Some years ago Dr. Francis Brown remarked that there are two classes of theologians, " those who think they know enough, and those who want to know more." When I speak of " our " Gospel, I am thinking of " those who want to know more," those who are loyal to the critical and historical method, accept the well-assured results of that method, adopt the principle of evolution as at least an indispensable hypothesis for men who would think in harmony with the science of our age, refuse to believe in a world of enchantment outside the world of experience, and will not admit that any doctrine of the church whatsoever has found its final statement.

Speaking to and for such men, I declare my conviction that the great religious need of to-day is that we should have a Gospel; that our worst weakness is the lack of a Gospel; that our greatest and most immediate duty is to find and proclaim our Gospel.

What do I mean by a Gospel? I mean a message that can not only hold its self-respect in the light of scientific thinking, but can prove itself a " power of God unto salvation." I mean a message that can rebuke, convict, and redeem a sinner; bring real comfort to a soul in sorrow; give assurance of hope in the face of death; put conquering strength into the tempted; and in short prove a practical power for human living.

Such a Gospel the religious world demands of us. So far we have been concerned too exclusively with critical and theological reconstruction. We were fighting in self-defense; there was no time for building houses or planting vineyards. Moreover the critical and theological investigation was a prerequisite of a clear Gospel message. But now the right to think the thoughts of to-day and stay inside the church is won. It is time we are taking our critical and theological reconstruction for granted, and going on to develop and proclaim the Gospel which alone can justify us in the eyes of the world.

For the world is a pragmatist in its taste. We can demonstrate—I think we have demonstrated—that our view of the Bible and of doctrine is truer and worthier than the old view. But this world looks for fruits. If we get and show for our painful and disturbing efforts no added power to comfort, strengthen, and save, no new vital message, no new tone of authority in proclaiming the old message, the world will continue to think of us as needless troublers of Israel. And the world will be right. The final test of what is taught in the Theological Seminaries is not its intellectual or ethical soundness, but the Gospel it inspires you and me to preach. The final test of your ministry and mine is its redeeming power in human life.

But a positive Gospel is demanded of us not only that we may justify ourselves, but as well that we may fulfill our mission. The world to-day needs a Gospel which only we, of the progressive wing of the church, can give.

Of course what is needed is not a new Gospel at all, but a new setting of the everlasting Gospel of our Lord Jesus Christ. We are all agreed upon that. We are not moving away from Christ; nor are we even going back to Christ; we are moving on with Christ. We have gone back to Him in our critical and theological studies, only that we may know Him better, and so follow Him more closely. But the world needs a new setting of His Gospel and a new vigor in proclaiming it; and we must meet that need or it will not be met. For only the men of modern viewpoint have the thought-foundation and the point of contact necessary for the proclamation of an effective Gospel.

I need spend no time trying to make evident the painfully clear fact that we are living in a new world. There is a social consciousness, a world-view, a craving for unity, an independence of thought and action, an industrial massing, that demands a new saving power, a new outbreaking of the Gospel; and how can we face this modern world, needing so painfully a religion fitted to it, and then look back over our training in fearless searching of the Bible, in open-minded desire for facts, in broad human interest, and not recognize the hand of God upon our spirits and the voice of God in our hearts, summoning us to give the world a Gospel which we do not hesitate to speak of as ours, just as Paul spoke of "our Gospel," "my Gospel."

There are many indications that the sense of need of a Gospel has been growing acute in the hearts of progressive men through the past few years. Not long ago, in a meeting of liberal men, something was said about "saving souls," and one of the leaders remarked: "I do not care about saving souls; all I want to do is to set the truth before men and leave them to deal with it." Some of us who, a few years back, would scarcely have criticized that attitude, now feel how grotesquely inadequate it is as the attitude of a minister toward his work. Unless the deepest desire of our hearts is to save men we have no business in the ministry of Jesus Christ. Of course "save" is to us a vastly bigger word than in the thought of past days, not tied up to a future heaven or hell, nor to a single instant of decision, nor to a special type of creed; but as big, broad and deep as life itself, as unbounded as Jesus' own redeeming work. But to be good ministers of Jesus Christ, and true helpers of the world, we must be at least as intense in our desire to save men in all ways as our fathers were to save them in the one way.

This deepening sense of the need of a Gospel has frequently proved a temptation. Realizing the urgent demand for a message of salvation, the present lack of a clear Gospel in harmony with our modern faith, and the attraction still residing in old phrases and methods, some have been led into an attempt to use old words and old ways, echoes of the dead past, despite the inherent contradiction between them and the real faith of their hearts. A man of modern type once said to me, "I know my theology is a great deal nearer the truth than my father's was. But I would give all my light for a little of his heat." Many of us have been so tempted, as Esau was; and some have yielded, as Esau did. It is a Faust-bargain, exchanging soul integrity for a temporary success.

With others the temptation has been to assume what is known as a "positive note" in preaching. I am thinking not of the true positiveness that means confident affirmation of our real faith, but the assumed positiveness, the violent assertion, the proclaiming "Thus saith the Lord," not because we believe that the Lord has said it, but because of the impression the assertion will produce. It is the method employed by a certain preacher, who remarked that when he came to a place in his argument where he felt weak, he "always hollered louder."

Against these and similar reactionary or shallow expedients, we must set a stern guard. We have put our hand to the plough; we art not fit for the Kingdom if we turn back. We must find our Gospel by moving forward, not by looking backward. With toil and pain, at any cost, we must work out the meaning and application of the Gospel to-day, and put our souls into the preaching and living of it.

What this is to mean in detail is a problem with which each of us must wrestle. And it is the mass of men out in the active ministry, not the leaders and teachers alone, who must work out the Gospel our world needs, the message that will grip the conscience, inspire the heart, command the will, dominate the life of the average man of our time, and, above all, impress him as spiritual and eternal in the vital sense of being real.

May I venture to indicate certain lines along which I believe we must move toward such a convincing Gospel message?

It will come not through hiding our faith, but through frank outspeaking.

There may have been a time, I think there was, when it was the part of wisdom and honor to say little directly and openly about the new views of truth, the new Bible which criticism had given us, the changed point of view in theology, to let the new light dawn quietly. But that time is past. Knowledge of the new truth is widely diffused though vague. We can, and we should, speak out, telling the plain people of the churches what the new light on truth is, and what changes it necessitates. We must not hide new light under old bushels, or grope in yesterday's wardrobe for veils to cover our faces, or serve new wine from old bottles. It is high time we were saying plainly what we think, not offensively, not attacking old systems if we can avoid it; but quietly, resolutely leaving old systems sidetracked, save where they insist on the right of way (in that case we must *keep* them sidetracked) and telling the people the truth of God in His world and in His word as we see it to-day. We need to follow Mark Twain's effective counsel, "When in doubt, tell the truth."

But will not this be dangerous? To ourselves, very likely. But it may be our Gospel will shine out the more clearly if we face misunderstanding for its sake. Will it be dangerous for the people who hear us? No. Not—and here is the gist of the matter—not if the people see plainly that our chief concern is not the maintaining of some particular theory, but their spiritual upbuilding. Where one would be unsettled or cast into doubt by plain preaching or modern thought, a score would be helped and led back into the way of God; and even the man made to doubt would be far better off than when comfortably settled in an inadequate faith. Paul's ideal should be ours: "Not walking in craftiness, nor handling the Word of God deceitfully; but by manifestation of the truth commending ourselves to every man's conscience in the sight of God." Plain preaching of that sort, throwing aside all thought of evasion or compromise, will help clear the way to our Gospel. This does not mean bringing critical conjectures or theological negations into the pulpit; it does mean stating in the plainest words we can find the faith in which our own hearts are living and rejoicing.

We should be able to discern and to show the spiritual value of our view of religious truth. We should cease apologizing for the modern view of truth, and begin to be missionaries, eagerly pointing out the incomparable values it possesses. We should adopt the method of the Epistle to the Hebrews, acknowledging the glory and power of the older faith, but pointing out with glowing zeal how much better is the new. Our critics assert that the new view makes the Bible and the Master less divine by making them more human. Let us glory in the fact that, by making the Bible more human, we make it more real and so more divine; and that, by making Jesus more human, we make Him more really Son of God. The new view of the Bible sets free an inestimable moral and religious force; for it shows us the heroes of Israel as "men of like passions with ourselves," struggling manfully out of their crude beliefs up to a true apprehension of the living God. Texts that were dead or sleeping in the old world of thought flash into splendid meaning in the new light. "That he might be the first-born among many brethren"; "the earnest expectation of the creation waiteth for the revealing of the sons of God"; how near Christ comes to us, and we to Him, in those great words; and that sort of nearness means power.

What a Gospel of Freedom we have to preach! The man who stands in the new light is not afraid that some new discovery, some novel theory, will knock the props from under his faith. His faith does not need props; the universe supports it. "Fear hath torment; but perfect love casteth out fear." Is not that great gain? Is there no worthy Gospel in the proclamation that the whole world of truth is open to one, without bolts or bars, with no enemies to fear? "God hath not given us the spirit of fear, but of power, and of love, and of a sound mind." What could the preacher of the older sort make of that text compared with the Gospel we find in it? With the critical and theological basis for faith that we have, you and I ought to be able to preach the love of God, the brotherhood of Christ, the reality of religion, the glory of following Jesus, the splendor of eternal life, the courage of faith, as no man ever preached them before. Let us awaken to the spiritual value of our own beliefs.

It is but viewing the same thing from another angle to say that we can and should emphasize the positive elements of the common faith. We have been critical and negative long enough. We have fallen into the fallacious fashion of attacking certain beliefs as non-essential. If they are non-essential, in heaven's name let them alone! Sometimes of course a non-essential must be attacked. Paul said, "Neither circumcision nor uncircumcision availeth anything"; yet on occasion he could strike hard at circumcision, when it was thrust forward as an essential. But we might well now leave non-essentials aside, and go on to emphasize the positive elements in Christian faith. If we do not believe in the crude substitutionary theory of the atonement, is that any excuse for giving our main attention to attacking the old theory? We do believe in the vicarious death, in a divine and all-pervading principle of sacrifice for the life of others, finding its most powerful and perfect expression in the life and death of Jesus; we do believe that His death has in it a saving, purifying force, whereby God redeems men. We see, as believers of the older type could not see it, the cross the believer must carry, the share of the disciple in the redemptive work of the Master. Preach that! Or if not that, preach what you do find in the cross, setting aside what you do not find there, and speaking gently if at all, of what to others seems sacred, even if to you it seem false or hurtful.

What a wealth of positive teaching and inspiration lies in unappropriated words of the Master and of the prophets and apostles about the Kingdom of God. Hard enthusiastic Bible study would endow many of us with a Gospel message. If some of us who are coldly criticizing evangelism,—perhaps with some justice,—would simply live with Amos and Isaiah, with Paul and James, above all with Jesus, till we caught their spirit, saw their social visions, and the applications they make of religion to our social relations, we could speak with a tongue of flame, and men would listen and be convicted of sin, and righteousness and judgment. When such an evangelistic message is heard from the pulpits as Professor Rauschenbusch has written, the world will feel itself in the presence of a Gospel that saves and condemns, and that speaks with the authority of God.

Most of all we can find our Gospel in the presentation of religion as a stern, high, life-demanding art. The religious world is cursed to-day with a soft and easy conception of the religious life, its origin, its maintenance, its destiny. The preacher has sought too exclusively such texts as "Come unto me and I will give you rest," neglecting the far more numerous words that tell of denying the self, taking up the cross, losing the life, being persecuted for righteousness' sake. Let ours be the Gospel of the straight gate and the narrow way.

With the new light from science, from a better understood revelation, from psychology, we can preach, as no man ever preached it before, the necessity of whole-souled religion, the demand of God for a united heart and an entire life, the challenge of Jesus to count the cost before becoming His disciple. Such a message the world has lacked these many years; and for lack of it the world has grown indifferent toward religion, thinking it a cheap thing. Such a Gospel we can give.

Seven years ago Dr. Theodore T. Munger wrote on "The Church. Some immediate Questions." There was a frankness almost overpowering in his words, as of a man at the end of life, with nothing to fear, and nothing to hide. He has given there a vision of our Gospel:

"The creed of life, if we may so term it, will be definite, searching, severe in its penalties and as relentless as they are in life itself, urgent both on the restrictions and the possibilities of life, and never forgetful of those inspirations that always come when the full meaning and import of life are revealed. Its sacrifice will be more real than that of a vicarious oblation, for it will be of self and on the cross of obedience to truth and duty. Its heaven will not be so clear and golden as that of old, but it will take on such color and form as overcoming life may give it, and become as real and present as life itself. The confusion of to-day will not be ended by blowing it away into mist, nor by explosions of criticism, but only by clear vision now opened by real life in a real world."

It is time we were finding our Gospel and proclaiming it. The world waits for it. Our training and labor come to nothing without it. We can find it, if we push forward with hearts filled with longing unrestrained to save men, to save the world. The sky is not wholly clear; but God still guides by a pillar of cloud. We can bring to the world the deeper religious experience, and the more real statement of truth it needs only as we ourselves find a deeper, richer experience of God than the faith of the past produced, and know its sources in ourselves so surely that we can reveal them to others. But all this can be only as our commanding passion is for saving men. "I preached as dying man to dying men," said Baxter. That is not our ideal. We want to preach as living man to living men. But we need the most solemn sense of responsibility and the glad conviction of the power of the Gospel that the men of Baxter's day felt so keenly.

Frederick W. Robertson, pioneer of the religion of to-day,

once voiced his ideal in words that may well guide our preaching:

" To live by trust in God,—to do and say the right because it is lovely; to dare to gaze on the splendor of naked truth, without putting a false veil before it to terrify children and old women by mystery and vagueness,—to live by love and not by fear; that is the life of a true brave man who will take Christ and His mind for the truth, instead of the clamor of either the worldly world or the religious world."

4.

The Christian Missionary and his Message in the Twentieth Century

By the Reverend President Howard S. Bliss, D.D.

MR. PRESIDENT AND FELLOW ALUMNI:

I realize that in having been chosen to speak at this time I have been chosen in somewhat of a representative capacity, and I wish on behalf of all my fellow missionaries in the foreign field, graduates of Union, to express our joy in this day and our gratitude for it. I gladly represent them in these words of felicitation. But in what I am about to say I am, of course, speaking my own thoughts, and my brethren must not be held responsible for what I may say. My theme is " The Christian Missionary in the Twentieth Century and his Message."

Man craves life. The craving is elemental and universal. It is life for which a man struggles more than for anything else. All his instincts are his allies in this conflict. It is because Jesus Christ came with a message that dealt with this supreme desire for life that Jesus' message is a world-message. He claimed to know how men might live and live adequately, fully, overflowingly; and He came not with words simply, but with a life that delivered His message even better than His words. He gave the impression of being alive, vigorously alive, overflowingly alive, alive with a life that defied poverty, hardship, disease, sorrow and death. Men asked Him the secret of it all, and He answered them in terms that all men could understand, for the terms were universal terms and dealt with universal facts. And the answer was surprisingly simple. Can we ever realize how simple it is? "If you wish to live," said Christ, "really live—not a life of mere existence, but a life of life, victorious, eternal—you must know God as your Father, wise, just, loving, strong; and you must love him with every ounce of your being. You must know yourself as God's child, docile, trustful, obedient; and you must love yourself as such. You must know your fellowman as your brother, and you must love him as you love your brother; and all this force which I have called love must be the kind of force which I have used in loving you; the love that expresses itself in service; the love that, having loved, loves to the very end. Do this, begin to do this, and you shall begin to live; you shall live, and live in such peace as the world cannot give, and possessed by a joy that nothing can take away from you." This simple message seems to me to be Christ's message, and this is the message he repeats to every man in the world as a man and every community as a community, to every nation as a nation—or would fain repeat it. And He says it with absolute assurance that the man who follows this programme will feel within himself a powerful spring of life, overflowing and victorious.

How will the man know it? He will know it—know it as the thirsty man knows that his thirst is quenched when once it is quenched; know it as the hungry man knows when his hunger is appeased; know it as a live man knows he is alive. He will know it. This, I repeat, is the essence of the message of Christ to the world, as I conceive it, drawn from the meagre and conflicting but sufficient accounts of that life that have come down to us and put into words that all men can understand. It may be variously expressed. But essentially it is the interpretation of the universe in terms of love. Many details might be added—but they are details, splendid details, but still details. Many questions might be started, and many, though not all, might be answered and answered with more or less profit to the questioner, but neither question nor answer is essential. Without them man's great craving for life that is life indeed, would be satisfied, and peace and joy would be his.

Much, however, of course remains implied. For the moment a man tries to follow this programme of Christ in his craving for the real, for the living God, in his desire to love God with every ounce of his being and to serve Him, he becomes that moment instantly aware of the difficulty of the task, of the impossibility of the task without the helping hand of the loving God. But that helping hand is a part of the simple message of Christ. Sin will rise up to block his way and put down his advances, or to stab him stealthily in the back, but there he will find God's helping, forgiving hand. A deeper note must be struck—the note of God's power. Without a realization of the fact that God's helping hand is not only loving and tender, but strong—strong for every emergency—man's effort will be a losing effort and the end will be defeat.

Now, of course, it is absolutely inevitable, as it is absolutely proper, that Christ's message, that Christ's interpretation of the universe, should be subjected to an intellectual re-statement as varied as the mind of man, a statement more elaborate and more closely articulated in its various parts than this simple statement from the lips of Jesus Christ. For His message, while expressed in this wonderfully simple fashion, deals with the greatest things in the world, the most mysterious, the deepest, the most baffling; and it is natural that man should wish to explore more closely and explain more minutely and justify more completely the message. Here there must be perfect liberty. Each temperament should be given its full freedom for speculation, for inference, for conjecture, for elaboration. I shall revert to this point because it is important; but here the plea must be made—with full recognition of the perennial honor in which the theologian must be held—that Christ's message must remain on the lips of every one of his messengers, simple in its assertions, ample in its outlines, universal in its terms.

Such being the message of the Christian missionary in the First Century, we may now proceed to draw some conclusions based upon this brief statement.

In the first place, it is evident that the message in its very nature necessitates the messenger—creates the messenger. Love, if it be love, must express itself. Christ's real commission to evangelize the world is not in the words spoken in His last hours upon the earth. His message is His commission, and the reason why the world has not long ago been evangelized is because somewhere in the long line of descendants from the early Christians the message failed to be really received. All this means, if it means anything, that every Christian is perforce a missionary. We are indeed beginning to realize that all Christians are ministers, so the terms minister and missionary are interchangeable, and as to the word foreign, as applied to missionaries, useful and necessary as the adjective may be from administrative or geographical considerations, it becomes a mischievous, impertinent and dangerous word if it arrogates to itself the right of a qualitative distinction in this connection. It remains true, however, that the missionary laboring in foreign soil or the missionary laboring at home in America among foreign elements is confronted with a set of problems different from those which meet his fellow-workers in another field. This arises from the fact that generally he is dealing with men strongly committed to other beliefs, men whose mental processes are different from his own race, not simply individually but racially. He is usually speaking in a language imperfectly acquired, at the best inadequately assimilated. To these natural difficulties must be added the difficulties arising from hostility on the part of his constituency, from prejudice, from inherited misconception, from resentment at what seems to him like intrusion. Added to this, the missionary must often overcome the poisonous impressions left in the minds and hearts of the people among whom he is working by the blunders, by the cruelty, by the callous greed, by the selfish aggrandizement of the so-called Christian nations.

Ask Moslem Turkey to-day what she thinks of Christian Austria, and therefore of Christianity; ask the Jewish people what they think of Christian Russia, and therefore of Christianity; ask heathen Congo what it thinks of Christian Belgium, and therefore of Christianity; nay, ask millions of people in the Christian Russian Empire, with Tolstoy denied Christian burial, what they think of Christianity, and then realize the seriousness of the Christian Missionary's work upon foreign soil!

Secondly, the Christian missionary must realize that his message will have no meaning unless he himself is the product of the message, representing and living the life which he asserts is the true life, visualizing that life in his own experience and in his own activities, showing the great truths of the great programme of Christ. Never were Emerson's words more true than of the missionary, "What you are speaks so loud I cannot hear what you say." And here is found the practical difficulty, and here is the reason why the extension of Christ's kingdom has so pitifully halted, why nineteen hundred years after its proclamation hundreds of millions of people do not know that God is their Father, that man is their brother. The reason, I say, is that our own lives have not kept up with our own words; that we do not know really what we are talking about. "Speak *things*" cried Emerson, "or hold your tongue."

I believe that the real test of Christianity is coming with the facing of the race problem. We shall then know whether Christ's avowed followers really believe in the Brotherhood of Men.

In the third place, the Christian missionary in carrying the message to all the world, must insist that Christ's message is a definite and distinct message, based, as we believe, upon the knowledge of facts as facts. Christianity respects all that is good in Buddhism; but Christianity is not Buddhism. Christianity is not Brahmanism, it is not Mohammedanism, however near these religions may come in some of their teachings to the teachings of Christ. It is a Christian message, based upon a particular attitude to the universe, explicit, precise and unique. Men may reject it, and they have a right to reject it; but in rejecting it they must reject something that is a definite and coherent interpretation of the great mysteries surrounding us.

Fourthly, in carrying the message to all the world, the missionary, while carrying the message in its great simple outlines, must expect and must encourage the age in which he is living, or the people among whom he is dwelling, to work out in their own way the details of its interpretation. the details of the meaning of these great simple facts, very few in number, but going down into the deepest things in the universe.

I here revert to the point previously alluded to. In my judgment it cannot be too strongly emphasized, and emphasized with reference to every department of Christian thought and Christian activity, theological, ecclesiastical, liturgical and administrative, that there must be perfect liberty. This liberty must be insisted upon by the missionary as he realizes his great responsibility to those races and those people; and this liberty must be granted without recrimination, without reproach and without withdrawal.

Take such a practical question as the question of church organization. If you adopt any one of the familiar definitions of the Church, you will see what scope is given for local development according to the temper of the age, the necessities of the times, the traditions of the race. Here is Dexter's definition of the Church: "A Church is an association of the friends and followers of Christ, for the profession of the

Christian faith and the performance of Christian duty." But with even so simple a definition, what a host of questions at once crop up. How shall this association be organized? Who shall be the organizers, who the officers, what shall be the forms of admission, what the ritual?

The Christian missionary will be ready with his advice drawn from personal experience, based upon his historical reading; but he will be very careful how he attempts to control, or coerce or legislate. He will insist, on the other hand, that all these questions shall be worked out locally. For example, among the questions that occur will be that of baptism. Leave it to the local development. The question of the Lord's Supper, sacred and beautiful as it is, is another which must be left to local development.

Was Grenfell right or wrong when he told his parishioners that Christ was not the Lamb but the seal of God? Was he irreverent, or was he a true apostle?

Find universal terms if possible. If you cannot do this, find local terms for different localities. For example, water for drinking purposes is a universal term. If you go throughout the whole world with a glass of water in your hand, everywhere the thirsty man, whether he knows where you come from or believes in you, will believe in the water and will reach out for it. Thus they will understand when Christ speaks of Himself as the " Water of Life." He spoke of Himself as the Bread of Life. And yet there are millions of people who never saw bread, or ate bread, or know the meaning of bread. And they will not understand Christ's phrase. Eat bread in their presence and they will know it is food and then they will believe in it as a true symbol.

If Jesus had been born in Labrador it is inconceivable that His message to us would have been different, so far as its great interpretations are concerned. But it is just as inconceivable that He would have interpreted His message in the language He used in Palestine as it would be that He would have clothed His body in the garments of that land. Parables, similes and formulas would all have been changed—the permanent abiding element would have been His message about God as Father, man as brother, self as minister, all linked together in the kind of love with which he loved the world.

Had Paul been born a Confucian instead of a Jew, or a Buddhist or a Brahman, and had still yielded his allegiance in these far-off lands to Jesus, and dedicated his life to Him as his Lord and Saviour, the epistles might still have been written, but in how surprisingly changed a form would the everlasting gospel which he preached have been presented! What strange omissions of arguments which we have been led to think indispensable or all but indispensable! What strange additions in historical allusions! What a new world of illustration and simile and metaphor!

Temperament is a gift of God. Moulds and categories of thought are gifts of God. Red skins and yellow skins and brown skins are gifts of God as well as white skins. The Orient belongs to him, and the Occident, the North Pole and the South, and when the indefinitely varied forces of man's complex nature cry out for individual expression, it is fighting against God to fight against this demand of nature. Man is man wherever man is found, one and indivisible in his essential characteristics. But men are men wherever men are found, as rich in multiform variety of expression as they are in elemental unity.

God is still a jealous God, but God is jealous for things and not for words. He never was and He never will be jealous about names and phraseologies and formularies. Christ was never concerned about the outward honor paid Him. He did not yearn to be admired; He yearned to be followed. He wished man to come to Him, not as a Shrine but as a Door; not as a Goal but as a Highway; not as a Memorial Tablet, but as a window through which they could see something; not as something to be gazed at so much as the Light whereby men might see God and man and life and opportunity as Christ saw it.

What are your thoughts of Christ? Formulate them in any way you please, provided you retain the authority of His leadership.

Does he save you from your sin? Call Him Saviour!

Does he free you from the slavery of your passions? Call Him Redeemer!

Does He teach you as no one else has taught you? Call Him Teacher and Master!

Does He heal you from that which seemed to be an incurable disease? Call Him Physician!

Does He shine upon the pathway that is dark to you? Call Him Leader!

Does He reveal God to you? Call Him the Son of God!

Does He reveal man? Call Him the Son of Man!

Or, in following Him, are your lips silent in your incapacity to define Him and His power, and is your mouth dumb? Call Him nothing, but follow Him!

Oh, how our divisive names shrivel up and disappear in the presence of actual discipleship and under the realities of personal experience.

The Christian missionary must recognize this, and must recognize it not grudgingly but gladly. Tenacious of his own favorite formulation and insisting upon his right to that formulation, he will grant to others the same liberty he claims for himself. So far from deprecating variety he will welcome it as increasing the cogency of the appeal of the great gospel of Jesus Christ as it is presented to men of many races, many types of civilization and to many grades within those types. The old battle-cries which quickly drew swords from scabbards and set the Christian Church in battle array against itself, will become but the mottoes of the different regiments, fighting not against honest men's honest convictions, but against lust and pride and irreverence and hatred and falsity. The old words will not disappear, but they will lose their rancor; and Arminian and Socinian and Calvinist, Trinitarian and Unitarian, Roman Catholic and Greek Orthodox and Protestant, will be names that carry respect if not conviction because of the fact that they represent formulations of belief in matters ecclesiastical, theological and liturgical that best express for some group of Christians, if not for you, the Message of the Master.

And shall we not pray that long before these great and massive buildings of this particular School of the Prophets shall show signs of decay our Seminary shall enroll among its teachers and its students men of as varied forms of belief as the names which I have cited would indicate? Yes, we must open the doors wide, but we must be sure and have wide doors to open! For when Christ speaks of Himself as the Door, it is well that we shall so build our Seminary that its door shall not be narrower than the door which Christ himself represented.

The missionary must, furthermore, beware how he transmits to his constituency the historic creeds that have ceased to mean for him the things that they meant for their framers; have ceased perhaps in some of their articles to mean anything at all to him. Whatever justification a man may feel at home for continuing to repeat such words (and I for one think we are in great peril of sacrificing frankness and reality and even plain honesty with great ensuing loss of power, for men respect words that mean what they mean, in the interests of continuity with the great historic churches), abroad there must be some other way to preserve continuity. Otherwise a deadly blight must follow the discovery upon the part of the people with whom we work, that the solemn recital of *I believe* covers really a statement of what *I half believe,* or at most a belief that I would ordinarily express in very different words and phrases.

Do not misunderstand me. Back of every article of these venerable creeds there is presumably some great and important truth. I would not have the missionary neglect it, if it be indeed a part of the Message of Christ, but I would have him realize his obligation to restate the truth in meaningful words. At his own peril, and to the peril of his hearers, he will pass over to them words that to-day may be only infelicitous, but which to-morrow will become chains about their necks.

And this leads me to say that the missionary must beware of his vocabulary. He must realize the importance of pruning his dictionary from the standpoint of brotherly appreciation. He must also be careful of his words from the standpoint of theological development. Think of the burdens that have been laid upon workers among Moslems by the introduction of the word *person* in connection with the formulation of the doctrine of the Trinity, or by the all but universal use among Christians of the expression, " For Christ's sake." It may be helpful to you and you understand it, but cannot a term be found that does not suggest that God loves men less than Christ?

Mohammed in his early life came in contact with Christians, and yet somehow got the impression that the Trinity consisted of God the Father, God the Son, and the Virgin Mary. He somehow got the impression that God would answer prayer only when the saints had been asked to use their influence with Joseph, to use his influence with Mary, to use her influence with Jesus, to use His influence with God. I wish to speak in great and utter reverence. Mohammed could not find God in that way, and he had to find God. Mohammed had to have a God that was a nearer God, and he cried out of his heart-hunger and his heart-thirst, and he got his answer. God found him. God spoke to him. God said, " Mohammed, I am near to you; *I am nearer to you than the great artery of your neck.*"

The missionary must not adopt words or phrases, however convenient and easy of use, if thereby he runs the risk of confusing the minds of the coming generation, and thus misrepresenting the truth he would fain represent. The missionary must never forget that before he begins his work in the heart of a man, God has been already working in that heart; indeed, the great need of the missionary is to know that God cannot work with him unless he is working with God. The image of God, however blurred and worn and marred, is still in every man's heart. The light that lighteth every man that cometh into the world is still burning in the heart, however dimly. And hence the approach to that heart on the part of the missionary must be sympathetic, it must be tender, it must be appreciative. That man has some form of religion, and the religious impulse is always from God. It is shamefully distorted at times, devilishly twisted, but the impulse is from God. God has been working there, and we must work with Him in that human heart, softly breathing upon that ember, almost dead, until it glows again and after awhile bursts into a little flame.

We must therefore beware how we rail at that heathen and his religion, lest we rail at God. Such words as heathens, infidels, and heretics, are not happy words in such connection, and he had better drop them; also such a vocabulary as crusading against the foe. And besides, they do no good, but very great harm. The word *crusade* makes some of my Moslem students white with anger, and I do not wonder. We do not wish them to think of Christ, the meek and lowly Jesus, as coming armed as a crusader to overcome, in the fury of battle and the storm of slaughter, Mohammed and his followers. I have known men who are separated indefinitely from the gospel's influence just because of these infelicitous and these poisonous words. On the other hand, how richly beautiful is Christ's vocabulary in this connection: the seed, the light, the leaven, the life!

The missionary must approach his constituency intelligently. He must not underrate the task before him. He is not merely dealing with a sinful man, he is dealing with an ignorant man, or with a prejudiced man, or with a bigoted man, or a fanatical man, or he may be dealing with a man of great and profound intellect, and he must take these men seriously, he must acquaint himself with their religious creeds, and patiently and steadfastly must he strive to put himself into their minds and learn their logic.

Brethren, have I pictured an infallible man? Have I demanded unattainable qualifications? I have not done so purposely. I have tried to match men with opportunities, to meet a demand with an adequate supply. The picture has not been drawn in vain if it succeeds in shaming us out of our sloth, sobering us out of our easy good nature and quickening in us a new sense of the responsibilty we have assumed in undertaking to be known officially as the messengers of our Lord, charged with the proclamation of His message throughout the world. I would make the task so high, so exacting, so difficult, that our ablest, our most heroic, our most chivalrous youths, the most devoted in all our seats of learning, will be eager to be found worthy of being enrolled among these accredited messengers of Christ. I would make the Calling—one can ill spare this rich and meaningful word, compared with which the word profession seems to have a very meager content—I would make the Calling so rich and so full and so noble an undertaking and of such evident power for service that once again parents would dedicate at the cradle their sons to its high and severe and varied demands.

I have been speaking as a minister, as a missionary, as a foreign missionary; but before I close I must speak for a minute as a son of Union, our beloved Alma Mater. For us, my fellow-alumni, this day is indeed a day of high festival. We care not what the weather is outside; it is a day of bright and beautiful sunshine, and a time of holy omen for the oncoming kingdom of Christ in our lives, in our homes, in our parishes, in the world. Some of you may have shared my ignorance of Presbyterian history when, on entering the Seminary as a student, I entered it with the impression that the name Union represented an interdenominational theological Seminary. At the time I was mistaken, and the discovery of the mistake brought its disappointment and its regret, but the years have brought their changes, and all trace of disappointment has been wiped out, for now our beloved Seminary has ceased to represent in its name a noble but narrow victory of conflicting parties struggling in a provincial field, but, thank God, has indeed become the union of larger things, standing for a comprehension of all the churches, yes standing for the emphasis of the great brotherhood of man, yes, standing for the union between us and Christ and God!

It is this new Union we now hail and acclaim; new, not simply, not chiefly because of this noble pile of recently constructed buildings, so suggestive of all that is admirable in ancient architecture and all that is practical in modern equipment, but new because our beloved Alma Mater has turned her face resolutely towards the new day, not forgetting, indeed, that to-day is the child of yesterday, and also not forgetting that to-day is the parent of to-morrow!

May God bless her in her new career! May God bless her and keep her! May God cause His face to shine upon her, and may God give her His peace. AMEN.

VII

THE ADDRESSES AT THE DEDICATION SERVICE

1 The Presentation Address, by the President of the Board, Robert C. Ogden, LL.D.

2 The Response for the Faculty, by the Reverend President Francis Brown, D.D., LL.D.

3 The Dedication Address by the Senior Professor, the Reverend Charles Augustus Briggs, D.D., LL.D.

I.

The Presentation Address

By President Robert C. Ogden, LL.D.

On the seventeenth of November, 1908, friends of the Seminary joined with its Directors and Faculty in the exercises incidental to laying the corner stone of these buildings. On that occasion the Directors were represented by the President, Mr. John Crosby Brown, and the Building Committee by one of its members, the Reverend Professor George William Knox.

From that date onward the construction of the buildings went steadily forward in a successful and satisfactory manner, with only slight delays and without serious accident, until now the entire personnel of the Seminary, Students, Professors, President of the Faculty, and Executive Staff are comfortably installed in commodious, elegant and practically completed quarters and have fully entered upon the practical work of the seventy-fifth Academic Year of the Seminary. In the short space of two years a beautiful hope has passed from a creation of the imagination to an exquisite material expression.

We are now assembled that we may complete the transaction begun two years since and dedicate these buildings by appropriate religious service and suggestive public address to their sacred and holy purposes.

In recent years death has been busy with the ranks of our Board of Directors. Shortly after the laying of the corner stone our President, Mr. John Crosby Brown, passed over to the majority of our Associates already in the life beyond. I am thus called to stand in his place and to speak to you briefly in behalf of the Board of Directors and its Building Committee.

The occasion is in its very nature unique. The dedication of a great group of buildings exclusively to religious education is a very rare event. Structures devoted to science, the fine arts, religious worship, public service and education will in the future be numerous and their dedication not uncommon. Some are here present that witnessed on December 9th, 1884, the dedication of the buildings at No. 700 Park Avenue, but it is unthinkable that any of this audience will ever witness any departure of this Seminary from this place, or any change of construction beyond some additions already planned.

Some quite remarkable incidents have marked the construction of these buildings. Especially noticeable was the selection of the plans. In response to the invitation of the Building Committee, thirty-five architects and firms submitted plans. The authorship of the various designs was scrupulously concealed from the knowledge of every one. Under this condition a jury of architects was selected to examine all and advise upon the best. After this the Committee was assembled for the final decision. An extended personal examination followed and when an expression of preference was solicited the entire Committee was a unit upon the first choice. Upon opening the sealed verdict of the architects it was found to be the same as that of the Committee. This remarkable harmony and unity has supplied the keynote of the whole construction. The solemn element in the proceeding is that three members of that Building Committee have passed away, Mr. D. Willis James and the Reverend President Charles Cuthbert Hall before the laying of the corner stone and Mr. John Crosby Brown, afterward. The buildings stand here essentially complete upon the lines originally chosen. There has been no occasion to regret at any point the decision then made. May we not take the conditions under which this group of buildings has been created as a prophecy of the unity of spirit, the bonds of peace, the dynamic energy, under which this Seminary shall continue its future work, continually rising with the lengthening years to greater heights of powerful influence!

In organizations of every sort it is impossible to overestimate the value of spiritual life. This is true in varying degrees of business and academic corporations, of factories and of churches, and in the highest extent of institutions for religious education. This spirit is the product of individual lives and character. When an educational institution, and especially one founded for religious purposes, is rich in the heritage of accumulated forces produced by a great aggregate of great lives the administration of its affairs imposes a very solemn duty. Such is the case with this Seminary. From a study of the past there arises a group of memories, hallowed, sacred, inspiring—the roll-call of its nobility may be heard in the Court of Heaven and the whisperings of its echoes are often in our thoughts as their names are often on our lips—Butler, Dodge, Jesup, McAlpin, James, Brown, Adams, Hitchcock, Hall. The entire list is too long for repetition.

No academic heritage can be more intolerable than a financial debt to the past, but there is richness beyond the power of money to buy, in a spiritual debt to the past. Its inspiration can supply nerve to the weak arm, can give courage to the timid heart, can strengthen the tired brain. From the beginning, seventy-five years ago, continuously to this very hour, this debt of the Union Seminary has been accumulating. In counting up its assets we can find with every instance of large material generosity, that may be estimated in currency, a large gift of the spirit that makes a priceless contribution of faith and hope.

This occasion gives potential evidence of the close association of the material and the ideal existing in this institution. While our thoughts are busy with the munificence of Mr. James and later of Mrs. James, both supplemented by the liberality of Mr. Brown, we must not forget that we are occupied with the larger interests of a school of the Prophets of national and international reputation. In this Seminary the constructive note of progress takes its impulse from a living faith that is certain and from a spirit too genuine to be measured by words, but to be sought and to be found in the ideals of her godly sons.

The position of this Seminary has been wrought out through the stress and strain of conflict and misunderstanding with a spirit of tolerance such as she only desired to receive from others. After an extended period of reconstruction, the Seminary is now at a point where its mission is not controversy but reconciliation. The crowning official act came with the elimination of subscription to an ancient creed as the binding official symbol qualifying Directors and Faculty and the substitution therefor of a simple, clear, concise statement of evangelical faith in God and in his son Jesus Christ that could be acceptable to Christian believers of every name. That final step was longer and higher than appeared to many. But there were men of vision who saw more clearly the possibilities of that advance. Prominent among them were Mr. James, Mr. Brown and Dr. Hall, prophetic spirits, keen to discern the truth and courageous to express it. And this dedication of this great plant is the outcome of that action. We look at it with loving admiration, we name its cost in dollars, we accept it all with a certain honest gratitude and pride. But our larger response is for the sympathy of the human hearts that inspired it, that gave themselves with their gifts and thus have built into these walls, with a grace beyond the highest capacities of art to express, their own human lives.

We do not admit in this Seminary the truth of the proposition that there must be a secular side to a religious organization. By its very nature it is all sacred whether the transactions be in stocks, bonds, cash, real estate, the sacred scriptures, religious scholarship or any of the sorts of training for the ministry of the Holy Gospels.

Therefore in speaking officially for the Board of Directors I do not, in personally addressing you as the Reverend President Francis Brown, assume to speak from the secular to the sacred elements of this Seminary. In your own person the two forms of administration are united. You are a member of the Board of Directors, Chairman of its Executive Committee and President of the Faculty. It is in respect of this latter that I venture to speak a few words.

It is proper to congratulate you as the Executive head of this Seminary upon the occupancy of these admirable, complete and beautiful premises. I think I am correct in the statement that no essential has been omitted in their construction, although a few minor details await completion.

Appreciation from a cultivated Public of the appropriate elegance of the architecture of these buildings is coming to us in abundant measure. An increased number of appreciative students are responding to the opportunities of Christian scholarship offered by the Seminary. The open-minded spirit that marks the freedom of research prevailing here is generally recognized. The service rendered to sacred learning on behalf of all higher education in this country through the stand here taken for the liberty of the Gospels is gratefully acknowledged. All these points, and others not mentioned, material and intellectual, are prominent in our minds at this hour.

You are also to be congratulated that you are the head of an institution for religious education to which a young man may come from any Christian communion, enjoy all its advantages in scholarship and yet be entirely free from any proselyting influence. It is this spirit that unites five different denominations in the teaching staff and twenty in the student body. From this comes also the spirit of tolerance toward other and positively different faiths that seek to find the points of agreement for human betterment without putting undue emphasis upon points of difference.

And all this is quite consistent with our conviction that religious belief should be intelligent and positive, constructive not destructive, and that it should have competent, thoroughly equipped, courteous, kindly and tolerant defenders of the faith. To meet this condition it is well known is the purpose of yourself and your Faculty.

The forward movement inaugurated here to-day should, we think, mark a new and progressive epoch in theological education. It is not within the province of a layman even when speaking for a Board largely composed of clergymen, to give advice or even positive suggestion to the President of a Faculty. Nevertheless, I venture to remark that we are living in a period of change and expansion. It is necessary that Christianity should look toward the saving of society and of the State as well as of the individual, that the Fatherhood of God and the brotherhood of man imply in many human relations, and especially in religion, a democracy that should be essentially Christian. This great fact seems just now somewhat overshadowed.

To the plain man familiar with the ordinary affairs of life the present opportunity for the pastor seems never to have been equalled and the need for special training never so great. The exactions of complicated city life and the bare, hard conditions of rural life alike demand specific instruction. These suggestions, and others of equal import call for increasing attention that the mental and spiritual powers should combine the wisdom of the school with knowledge of practical affairs to the end that the Kingdom of God may come.

Knowing full well that you are leader and master in all subjects that pertain to your eminent position, that your ideals from the past and of the present are of the highest type, that you enjoy the affectionate allegiance of your faculty; I now, on behalf of your brothers in the Board of Directors confirm the loyalty expressed at your inauguration, two years ago, and with most ardent desires for your health, happiness, and long continued usefulness again commit the welfare of this Seminary to your care and keeping.

2.

The Response for the Faculty

By the Reverend President Francis Brown, D.D., LL.D.

MR. OGDEN:

It is a great trust which you are committing to the Faculty of this Seminary, whose spokesman I am permitted to be this afternoon. We thank you, and the Board of Directors, and its Building Committee, through you. We thank you for all the arrangements made so thoughtfully for our personal convenience. These are obvious to every visitor, and we have reason to appreciate them a hundred times a day. This is worth mentioning here, only because it makes for our efficiency as workmen, and we thank you, most of all, for the facilities with which you have here provided us to do the work you have set us to do. Our students share these feelings with us, and we are sorry that the limits of room make it impossible for all to be here, to show their enthusiasm, of which we have constant testimony.

We are all the more grateful because we understand quite well that you do not offer us these buildings that we may take our ease in them, but that we may render larger service in them. You are not spreading cushions for us to repose on. You are opening a door into a broader field. You are not setting us on this hill-top that we may be conspicuous objects of envy as we bask in the sunshine of a new prosperity, but that we may join hands with our good neighbors who are here already in the advancement of knowledge and of personal power—and that we may look out more widely over the world, and train our cadets in view of the whole vast battle-field. We thank you for this splendid opportunity.

The trust comes to us with the authority of an imperative. These stones have voices and cry their summons to us. We are stupid and unworthy if we do not hear it. What are we to do with these buildings and *in* them? How are we to use this great vantage ground? The trust—in some ways unparalleled—imposes its tremendous obligation.

It is an obligation to the benefactors who have made this day possible. We cherish their names and feel our debt to them in our hearts. We are bound to see to it that their gifts accomplish in fact what they have so ardently wished them to accomplish.

It is an obligation to all our past, from the first group of Christian men who outlined this Seminary in their faithful plan—Absalom Peters, Henry White, William Patton, Erskine Mason, William Adams, and other ministers with them—Knowles Taylor, Richard T. Haines, William M. Halstead, Charles Butler, Fisher Howe, Norman White, Anson G. Phelps, and other laymen with them—from this group on through the strong Directors and wise teachers who gave the first tone, the distinct quality, to the Seminary, down to those who have only now left us, and those who are with us still. Mr. Ogden has spoken of our spiritual debt to the past. All these men who have put their good lives into the work of the Seminary—not without toil and strain—are our creditors, steadily insistent—not to withdraw their investment—they could not if they would, it had already been transformed into spiritual power—but to see their investment of life and thought and faith yielding its increment to the end, and this, just now, depends on our administration of the trust.

But our obligation is also to the Church of Christ. The Seminary has been established and cherished to serve the Church; its Directors, Professors and Graduates are servants of the Churches. The Church needs training for its servants and an institution like this is set to give it—training first for those whose one occupation is church leadership and activity, and then for those who seek fitness for some other special function in the Church's life. If we do not do this thing for those who come to us, we are failures, we are in the way, we are cumberers of the ground. To make the fit ones fitter, and to keep the unfit out, as far as in us lies, are the two aspects of this great obligation—and the Church ought to hold us to account—and inevitably, and almost unconsciously it does and it will. And this is a sobering matter for us to think about.

Among our superior obligations is the obligation to the truth. We feel bound to take this very seriously. It means that we must get at the truth, ourselves, to the limit of our power, and we do not imagine that we know it all, or ever shall. Necessity is upon us—a divine compulsion we think it is—to search after new aspects of truth, and to teach our students to do the same. We find the old truths unfolding into new meaning when we regard them, not as solid blocks, laid in cement, hard and changeless, but as a garden of plants and trees with perennial life, whose blossom and fruitage the watchful gaze can see. And because we know we can keep our eyes on only one side of the garden, we are glad to know that other observers have stationed themselves at other points, and we expect what they see to supplement what we see, and contribute to the rounded and completed truth. And our obligation is to see straight, and help our younger brothers who come to us for guidance to see straight—with their eyes, not with ours—because, so it seems to us, only the man who is ready to see the truth for himself, is prepared to know God.

Our supreme obligation is to God, our Father. The sacredness of all this great equipment, to which Mr. Ogden has alluded, makes the crowning duty for us. We know that we belong to God, and we believe that He belongs to us—"Our Father" we say. That means that the buildings and facilities entrusted to us are a commission from Him. Each man and woman of you has a sacred commission; this one is ours. We have to accept it at His hands, and discharge it, if we can.

Our God has shown Himself to us by many tokens, but chiefly in Jesus Christ—so that we are confident that God, who is Lord of all, in character and purpose is what Jesus showed himself to be—as righteous and wise and loving and forgiving and more, and stronger, because human and earthly conditions were present in Jesus which do not hamper God—that as much of God was in Jesus as a human life can show. And when we see Jesus giving himself for men, we know that God realizes his own desire in giving himself for men, and we see no final hope for men—no other deliverance from selfishness and obedience to the lower impulses—except in sharing this spirit, and adopting for themselves this divine plan of life which Jesus lived by, and which dwells forever in God. And our summons is to teach our students this. This means, of course, enlisting them intelligently in the service of spreading this spirit and manner of life in the earth. For this service they need knowledge of the world itself in its varied life and need, and some understanding of how the things that are have come to be. And they need long training in the art of applying their knowledge of God, which is meant for use in the common ways of men, to the actual problems—the intricate questions that vex weary hearts and proud hearts as the earth daily turns each face to the sun again, waking the sleepers once more to their old temptations and duties and opportunities.

It is a world-wide enterprise. Men in all continents have to learn the new lesson. And no man can work out his problem alone. We are born into families, and the whole world is akin, and to live with God means to live as members of the social organism, which God has set going, and in which his mighty plan is to be realized.

When we catch sight, as we do now and then, of that which is to be, we see men and women living everywhere in purity and peace, the strong bearing the infirmities of the weak and not pleasing themselves—pleasing themselves by serving the rest—a social life which is a life of righteousness and consideration in equal parts, and a heaven above to which ladders rise, with angels ascending and descending on every hand. The time is not yet—but we take it as the best expression of our obligation to God for these splendid things about us, that we devote ourselves as we accept this trust, devote ourselves with all we have, including what is lent to us so generously here, with all that we are, and can do, to patient work toward this one end—the reproduction of the character and purpose of our Lord Jesus Christ, which shall usher in the triumphant kingdom of God.

3.

The Dedication Address

The Ideal of the Study of Theology

By the Reverend Professor Charles Augustus Briggs, D.D., D.Litt.

We are assembled on this occasion to dedicate the new buildings of Union Theological Seminary to their work of training theological students for the Christian ministry. This is the third set of buildings in which this Seminary has been housed. It has been the privilege of the speaker to have been a student in the earliest of them, and a professor for thirty-six years in all of them. One of his chief joys is the friendship of the sometime President, Charles Butler, our venerable leader in troublous times, who linked the Founders with the present. It has also been his privilege to know by personal acquaintance several other Founders of this Seminary, and the most of its Directors, Professors and benefactors. On this occasion many of you are asking, what is the purpose of these splendid and costly buildings, erected by the piety and munificence of representative merchants of this metropolis. It is only fitting that I should answer you; and I am happy to be able to do so by simply unfolding the ideal of the Founders of the Seminary, to which each succeeding generation of Directors and Faculty has been faithful, as the charter of our duty and our rights, the exponent of the spirit and life of the Seminary, to be perpetuated in all time, the Ideal of the Study of Theology.

As I ask your attention to this theme to-day, I do so not merely out of reverence for the past, piety to the Founders, and fidelity to those noble men with whom I have been associated for so many years in this institution; but because my experience as a student and teacher of Theology for half a century, my studies in the history of theological education, and my acquaintance with institutions of learning in many parts of the world, all convince me that our Founders were altogether right in their ideal. I can subscribe to it, as I doubt not is the case with all my colleagues, with my whole heart.

It is an ideal so simple and yet so profound, so masterly and yet so inviting, that we and our predecessors have been trying to realize it during three-quarters of a century; in which this Seminary has risen, as it were from dust and ashes, through many sad experiences of poverty and affliction, of conflict, temporary defeat and ultimate victory, to our present magnificent situation.

We have not yet attained the fulness of our ideal, but in this new home, where we have such great opportunities for growth and expansion, excelling all that we had any right to expect, we are pressing on, with a more solemn realization of our privileges, but with fresh vigor and renewed courage, " toward the mark, for the prize of the high calling of God in Christ Jesus " (Phil. iii: 13–14); for we are assured that that mark is the Ideal of the Study of Theology.

Sadness tempers our joy as we remember those noble Directors who have so recently been taken from us: our late vice-president, D. Willis James, whose princely gifts first made these buildings possible; and our late president, John Crosby Brown, whose wise administration adopted their plans and laid their foundations; our Moses and Aaron, they saw the promised land from afar, and led us to its very gates, but were not permitted to enter. They are doubtless with us to-day, in spirit, and ever will be, as we endeavor to carry on the ideal of the Founders as they received it and embodied it for us in such worthy and appropriate structures.

The Ideal of Theological Education given us by our Founders in the Preamble of our Constitution is as follows:

"Being fully persuaded that vital godliness well-proved, a thorough education, and a wholesome practical training in works of benevolence and pastoral labors, are all essentially necessary to meet the wants and promote the best interests of the Kingdom of Christ, the Founders of this Seminary design that its students shall have the opportunity of adding to solid learning and true piety, enlightened experience."

This Preamble gives us three constituent elements of our ideal:

1—Vital godliness—true piety.

2—Thorough education—solid learning.

3—Wholesome practical training—enlightened experience.

The ideal of theological education of this Seminary is not that of all theological institutions, or of all teachers of theology. There are some who think these constituents inharmonious and inconsistent. There are many, especially in Germany, who regard the practical training as irreconcilable with a thorough scientific education; for, say they, the practical training, with the ministry of the Church in view, limits the study of theology to that which the Church requires, and makes the Church the final aim rather than the Truth itself. How can a scholar give himself to the search for the Truth, the whole Truth and nothing but the Truth, when the Church has already decided for him what the Truth is; and has indeed limited him to the denominational form of it, in his teaching and in his learning? This peril was fully understood by our Founders and wisely provided for. They say:

"It is the design of the Founders to provide a Theological Seminary in the midst of the greatest and most growing community of America, around which all men of moderate views and feelings, who desire to live free from party strife, and to stand aloof from all extremes of doctrinal speculation, practical radicalism and ecclesiastical domination, may cordially and affectionately rally."

They saw at the time of the founding of this Seminary that the then existing Theological Seminaries, for the most part, were subject to *ecclesiastical domination,* and were suffering from the evil effects of it. They saw very clearly that any action of ecclesiastical bodies, either in the appointment or removal of professors, or in the oversight, direction or criticism of their instruction, can only be destructive of theological scholarship. They were determined that this Seminary should never be subject to such control; and therefore it was organized by ministers and laymen entirely apart from any ecclesiastical body. They obtained a Charter from the State of New York which perpetuated the control of the Seminary by themselves and their successors chosen by themselves. The Directors of the Seminary in 1870, in the interests of the reunion of the Presbyterian Church and to relieve the other Seminaries of that Church from ecclesiastical domination, agreed to give the General Assembly the right of veto on the appointment of our Professors. But in 1891, when the General Assembly used this right of veto in an effort to gain ecclesiastical dominion over the Seminary, it was stoutly resisted, and it was soon ascertained that the Directors had transcended their charter rights and duties, even in giving the right of veto to the General Assembly.

Thus this Seminary was founded *free from ecclesiastical domination,* and it has fought a hard but victorious fight against it. The result of that battle has been a still further advance towards the ideal of the Founders.

As the Seminary was founded by Presbyterians, it was a part of the plan that the instruction should embrace "a thorough knowledge of the standards of faith and discipline of the Presbyterian Church." But it is evident that the Founders did not mean to lay stress upon this, for it was subordinated to the greater whole of "a full and thorough education," in which it was embraced as a part only. And in the Charter it is defined that "equal privileges of admission and instruction with all the advantages of the Institution, shall be allowed to students of every denomination of Christians." This provision involved that the teaching of these students should not be denominational teaching; but a teaching which all students of all denominations might attend with profit, and without detriment to their denominational affinities. And I can testify both as a student and a professor familiar with this Seminary for the greater part of its history that the instruction has always been of a comprehensive character without denominational bias. This attitude of the Seminary has been appropriately expressed in the name Union, and the Directors and Professors of this institution have ever been in the forefront of every movement for religious co-operation and reunion.

The requirement of special instruction "in the standards of the Presbyterian Church" implied as its complement—if "equal privileges" were to be allowed to students of every denomination of Christians—that the standards of all these denominations should also be studied. The Directors of the Seminary, by their generous but mistaken action of granting a veto over the appointment of their professors to the General Assembly of the Presbyterian Church, were prevented for twenty years from making any further advance towards their ideal. But soon after the rescinding of that act the Seminary opened its doors, not only to students, but to Professors and Directors from the different denominations. Five denominations of Christians are represented in our Faculty and Board of Directors, and the standards of the different denominations are taught by representatives of those denominations on a footing of perfect equality with the teaching of the standards of the Presbyterian Church. Thus Union Seminary carried out its ideal, by ruling out *denominationalism* as well as ecclesiastical domination.

These wise men went still further. They saw the evils that partisanship and party strife had brought upon the Presbyterian Church, and also upon other American Churches, by its interminable conflicts and divisions; and they were determined to separate this Seminary from them. Their ideal of the Seminary as expressed in our Preamble was that it should be one "around which all men of moderate views and feelings, who desire to live free from party strife may cordially and affectionately rally."

It must be said that this Seminary has never been partisan. It has never committed itself to any party in the Presbyterian Church or in any other Church. Its professors have been chiefly independent men, differing often in their views of doctrine and order. The students have indeed heard diverse opinions on the same subject in different class rooms. The students have been trained to think for themselves, to form their own opinions. No pressure has ever, so far as I know, been put upon them to adopt the opinion of any one Professor rather than of another. And no student has been influenced to change his ecclesiastical position, or his attitude to any burning question in the Church. The Professors have worked in harmony with mutual respect and recognition of differences. The teaching in this Seminary has ever been free from party strife, and the Professors have been usually moderate in the expression of their views and feelings. There have been times when it has been difficult to be moderate, and I cannot say that I or others have always been as temperate as we should have been. But I can affirm that the Seminary, as a body, and in all its official acts, has been faithful to the ideal of moderation of our Founders.

The Seminary has not escaped from conflict. It has been obliged to defend itself against wanton attacks, and its Professors have been forced into ecclesiastical contests of more or less severity, from the foundation of the Seminary to the present time. But such conflicts have not in the least turned the Seminary from its great ideals of moderation, peace and unity. We stand for these things to-day, just as we have always done.

Everyone who knows our history must say that the Directors of this Seminary have stood manfully by the Faculty for the rights of Christian scholarship and for the free untrammeled search for the Truth, and they have not abandoned in any respect their practical aims. The three constituent elements of theological education are not inconsistent, but complementary. Personal piety, the Truth for the Truth's sake, and the service of the Church are unified in God, our Creator and Saviour. Theology can have no other final aim than God Himself, communion with God, knowledge of God, and the service of God.

1. True Piety

"True Piety" or "Vital godliness well proved" is the fundamental and most essential element in the study of Theology. Our junior Professor was entirely correct when in answer to the question: "Can Religion be taught?" he said in his Inaugural Address:

"Only a mind that is already religious can be taught religion. A teacher cannot impart any absolutely new interest into the mind; he can only intensify an interest already there, or extend the application of it. Aristotle is right: the teaching of virtue presupposes virtue in the pupil, and the teaching of religion presupposes religion in the pupil."

So our great theologian Henry B. Smith said many years ago: "A true religion and a true theology are, in advanced culture, inseparable. True religion cannot be preserved without a true theology; nor can there be a vital theology without a vital religious experience." (*Introduction to the Study of Theology*, p. 55.)

And both reiterate the words of St. Paul, "The natural man receiveth not the things of the Spirit of God, for they are foolishness unto him; neither can he know because they are spiritually discerned." (I. Cor. ii: 14.)

Theological education like all higher education presupposes preparatory studies. The theological student must be prepared in vital religion as well as in knowledge. He comes to the study of theology with the scholar's degree, or its equivalent, which he has earned by long and patient study. But even more essential than that, he comes with "vital godliness well proved" and attested by credible evidence. Only such a man is competent for a student of theology.

The Theological Seminary has as one of its aims, the development of vital piety. This is one of the reasons why Theological Seminaries were established apart from and independent of Universities, because the study of theology in the University tends to become merely intellectual and scholastic. The provisions necessary for the development of that kind and degree of Christian piety necessary to the Christian minister are not so easily made, where the theological students are in the minority in a mass of all kinds and conditions of man, as where they are kept apart by themselves. These evils are not imaginary but real. The Church has suffered from them many times in its history, especially in the scholastic period of the Middle Ages and in the scholastic period of Protestantism.

The Council of Trent saw the necessity for the education of candidates for the ministry in Seminaries apart from the Universities, and by this provision did much to save the Roman Catholic Church from ruin, and bring about what is known as the Counter Reformation. So the Protestant Churches of Germany, Great Britain, and America have been obliged to organize Theological Seminaries to do that which the Universities did not or could not do—give the practical training necessary for the ministry of the Church.

But, if there are perils in the study of theology in the Universities, there are perils just as great in the isolation of theologians in Theological Seminaries. It is recognized by many of the best scholars in the Roman Church that the isolation of theological students has produced a multitude of evils. It is really the introduction of monastic methods for the training of the secular priesthood. It takes them out of the world for a series of years, but it makes it difficult for them ever to return to their lifework in the world. A Roman Catholic scholar recently told me that he came back to America, after many years of such isolation in Rome, and found himself altogether unprepared for the simplest things in the work of a parish priest. Such a training may develop an ascetic type of piety, but it does not and cannot develop that practical type of piety which is necessary for leadership in the religious life of the world.

The Protestant Theological Seminaries have not gone to such extremes as the Roman Catholic, but not a few of them have gone far in that direction, and it should be said that the isolation of the Theological Seminary ever tends towards a self-centered piety and one of a mechanical institutional type.

There are several kinds of piety, originating in the religious experiences of the several different temperaments which distinguish mankind. There are differences in piety due to the experience of families, of religious denominations, of nations and even of races. There is no other perfect piety than that of Jesus Christ our Saviour, whose piety was at once so simple and so comprehensive that it may be said to embrace all types in harmonious union. But that cannot be said of his apostles, or of the ministry and people of the Church in any age of the world. We all have our own special temperaments and experiences. These inevitably produce differences in piety, which cannot be pressed into any one mould, without serious injury to the growth of the divine life, in the soul of man, and in his activities in the world. The tendency of Seminaries is to assume a special type of doctrine, so also to manifest a peculiar type of piety. Both alike are injurious, the one to the scholar's quest for Truth, the other to the Christian's life in God.

The Founders of this Seminary saw these evils in the Theological Seminaries of their day, and they devised a very excellent method of overcoming them. Listen to their wise words.

"The Founders of this Seminary design that its students, living and acting under *pastoral influence* and performing the important duties of church members in *the several churches* to *which they belong,* or with which they worship, in the prayer-meetings, in the instruction of Sabbath schools and Bible classes, and being conversant with all social benevolent efforts in this important location, shall have the opportunity of adding to solid learning and true piety, enlightened experience."

This Seminary was in its original design, not separated from the world, but deliberately and intelligently planted "in the midst of the greatest and most growing community in America"; and this for the very purpose that Faculty and students should take an active part in the religious life of the city, and that their piety should grow in its practical exercise in all kinds of religious work.

The Seminary does indeed make provision for the development of the piety of the Faculty and students, in daily and weekly exercises of various kinds, some conducted by the Faculty, others organized and conducted by the students themselves; all of which, I am glad to say, are entirely voluntary and none of which are required. And so there is every opportunity for the development of piety without any pressure to conform to any special type.

But the Seminary still adheres to the ideal of our Founders that the best religious training is to be attained not in the isolation of the Seminary, but in the religious life of the city, under the supervision of the pastors of our city churches and the leaders in all kinds of religious and benevolent service. The students have the same liberty of choice here, as in other departments, as to the church with which they will worship, and the kind of work they will do, and the nature of the religious exercises they will undertake; but this is an essential part of their study.

Union Theological Seminary is not isolated from the great world, but it is in it, and rejoices to be of it; and yet we may retire from the world as much as we please, and in our own Seminary, consecrated by so many hallowed associations, we may be as mystic as we wish, or ascetic, as anyone will, without hindrance from anyone or anything. The most marked features of the alumni of this Seminary is that they are *Christian workers.* Their piety is of a practical kind, and yet we have had among them *mystics* of the best type, such as the Missionary Bowen of India, and our late President, Charles Cuthbert Hall.

2. *Full and Thorough Education—Solid Learning*

These are the terms that our Founders used to indicate what they meant by theological scholarship. They meant by "*thorough*" an education that was entire and complete, as opposed to an incomplete and partial education advocated by some as alone important for the practical work of the ministry. And so they say: "In all the subjects taught in the best Theological Seminaries in the United States." They designed this Seminary to be one of the best of its kind. They meant by "solid learning," learning that is the result of careful, painstaking, scholarly investigation, that is firmly embedded in the rock of eternal truth—*Solid* learning, that is, as they say, "aloof from all extremes of doctrinal speculation."

The greatest curse of theological scholarship is the "extremes of doctrinal speculation." These have always made mischief in the Church. They have urged the Church to premature scholastic definitions of doctrine in order to exclude them, which, while trying to mediate between the extremes, yet became themselves doctrinal speculations. These extremes have brought about almost all of the religious wars of Christian history, and have ever produced most serious evils to Christian scholarship, which often has been crushed between their upper and nether millstones.

Speculation has its proper place and importance in Theology as in other departments of human knowledge; but it is only proper when it builds on the solid rock of the most thorough knowledge thus far attained, in order to reach out towards the unapproachable and unknown. It is the cheap and easy way of the speculator to jump at his conclusions and to mock at the patient plodding scholar, who builds up his material by the use of all the resources of sound methods. He springs lightly over the obstacles that lie in his way until at last, with incautious self-confidence, he stumbles over something unobserved, and falls into the pit of destruction. A little patience with speculators and they destroy themselves.

I shall not say that all of our Professors have always kept themselves free from such speculations. But I do affirm that this Seminary as a body has stood firmly by the Preamble in this respect as well as in others, and that sound scholarship has been the characteristic of our institution. In the early days of this Seminary instruction was as *full* as it was practicable to make it, with the limited number of Professors; and the Faculty and students were quite as industrious as they are at present.

Edward Robinson gave this Seminary a reputation for Biblical scholarship that it has never lost. Henry Boynton Smith and Roswell D. Hitchcock advanced the study of Church History to the high level it has ever since maintained. When Henry B. Smith undertook the Chair of Systematic Theology he made Faith and Philosophy inseparable and christologized the entire system of Christian doctrine. Thomas H. Skinner led the choir of saintly men, William Adams, George Prentiss and Thomas S. Hastings, who enveloped Practical Theology with a halo of glory. Time would fail if I were to attempt to tell all that the Faculty of this Seminary has done for Theology, as in linked succession they have striven, often in poverty and affliction, to realize our Ideal of Theology, as it has gradually unfolded into larger, fuller and more comprehensive ranges of study.

The field of Theology is now so vast that it is impossible to cover it in the course of three years' study. The number of years of study is no greater now that we have twenty-one teachers than seventy years ago when we had but four. We are obliged to make the greater part of our teaching elective. There are many evils involved in this situation just as there are in the elective systems of the Colleges and the Universities. It is difficult to draw the line properly between what is elective and what is required. It is easier to make all elective or all required than to pursue the middle course.

The elective system encourages students to take the easier and more interesting courses and to neglect those that are difficult and technical; it invites him to specialize without sufficient general knowledge to enable him to specialize aright; it inclines him to the exaggeration of those things in which he is especially interested and the depreciation of everything else. And so it encourages the Professor to make his courses interesting to the student by the undue use of rhetoric at the expense of logic; it invites him to lecture upon subjects in which he is personally interested rather than upon those that will be most useful to the student; and it inclines him to overlap and intrude upon other departments, and to overlook and disregard the unity, harmony and proper proportions of the different departments of study.

There can be little doubt that, in the required courses of half a century ago, the student had usually a more comprehensive outline knowledge of Theology than he can obtain to-day by even the wisest selection of the electives. But on the other hand there were serious omissions, and inadequate and disproportionate treatment, in those days, even in the best institutions. It was necessary for all who wished to make any thorough study of theology to go to the universities of Europe for that purpose. At the present time, in Union Seminary at least, the field of Theology is as completely covered as in any university of Europe; and every method of instruction used whether in Germany, France, Great Britain or America, is employed by one or more of our professors. We combine the use of text books and lectures, the tutorial method of the English Universities with the Seminar method of the Germans; the popular lecture of the French with the technical of the Dutch.

The field of study is, however, so vast that it is no longer possible for the theological student to get an adequate knowledge of Theology in a three years' course. The time required for the study of Theology has not been increased for more than a century. In the meantime the legal and medical faculties have increased their requirements in time as well as in courses of study.

Union Seminary has within recent years organized a Graduate School of Theology, in which resident students and non-resident pastors of the neighborhood may continue their studies one, two, three, four years or more with the opportunity of winning a doctor's degree in Theology by outstanding merit.

Thus we are striving to rise to the heights of our ideal; and yet, I must say, that in many things we still fall short. Our present splendid plant with all its increased opportunities is none too large. We need additions to our Graduate Faculty, a large increase in our Library and endowments of fellowships for extended study and research. Theology still abides and will ever remain the supreme knowledge, for it is the knowledge of God and of all things in relation to God. It uses the methods and results of Science and Philosophy to sum them up in the comprehensive ideas of Theology. It has a Canon Law and a pastoral medicine which have unfolded in parallel lines with the Civil Law and Medical Science. As a late theologian of Glasgow so well says:

" No knowledge in any of its kinds or forms is, or can be, alien to theology as the Science of God. For He knows all and is known in all, and rightly interpreted, all knowledge is knowledge of Him. It is just the function of Theology to *theologize knowledge, to give it its last and highest expression in terms of God.*" (Hastie, *Introd.*, p. 45.)

3. A Wholesale Practical Training

The study of Theology, as the study of Law and Medicine, is not only theoretical but practical. It not only has in view the quest for truth and fact, but it also has the still higher aim of using the facts and putting the truth in practice. The Faculty of Medicine supplement their teaching by clinics and service in hospitals. The Faculty of Law add to legal learning, the experience of moot courts and service under approved lawyers, before admission to the bar. So the Theological Faculty add to their teaching, practical exercises for the training of the intending minister in all those activities which are necessary for the work of the Church.

Experience teaches us that while there is peril with some students that they may be distracted from their scholarly work by practical training, the peril is in many cases the other way. It is sometimes difficult to induce students to attend to this practical training especially when it is made optional. Nothing is more needed than hard study and technical discipline in wholesome combination. Long years of study in school and college make it easy and natural for the theological student to pursue his scholarly studies; but the practical training is, in large part at least, something new and difficult, which he does not care to undertake until he is convinced of its necessity.

Our Founders wisely provided for this practical training which they determined should be "*wholesome,*" because they wished to resist and overcome that "*practical radicalism*" which is the bane of all religious work. The Founders were well-known patrons of religious revivals, but they were opposed to that radicalism which in their days would make revivals the substitutes for the regular work of the Church. They were patrons of all kinds of religious and benevolent institutions designed to supplement and render religious activities more comprehensive; but they were opposed to that radicalism which would substitute any of these for the historic work of the Christian ministry.

When we consider what the Christian minister really has to do in the practice of Theology, we are overwhelmed with the amount of labor necessary to give that "wholesome practical training" that he needs.

The Christian minister is the representative of Jesus Christ in his offices of prophet, priest and king; and is at once a Church governor, a pastor, and a preacher. As a church governor, he must practice ecclesiastical law, and be the counsellor of his people in all matters of religion; and he must be prepared to plead at the bar of ecclesiastical courts, or sit therein as a judge of the most important matters. As a pastor he must go about from house to house to administer pastoral medicine, and he must conduct the worship of the people and administer the sacraments for their soul's good. As a prophet he has to teach in public and in private, dealing with all classes and ages in every grade of intellectual advancement, and adapt his teaching to the capacity of all. He needs all the resources of logic, rhetoric and oratory to stir the religious emotions of his people, persuade them to action, and lead them in those duties and privileges necessary to the development of their Christian life. He must furthermore be a man of affairs, of some executive ability, with sound judgment and nice discrimination in the common affairs of life. He must interest himself in every movement for good—political, social, economical, educational—that will improve the condition of his people. He must have sufficient general culture to prevent him from mistakes in his discourses or in his conversation upon the topics of the day. He should know something of church architecture, music, instrumental and vocal; and of choice literature; and in many religious bodies also, of painting and sculpture, and instruct in their religious uses.

Who is sufficient for these things? How is it possible for any man to be such a comprehensive thinker and worker—lawyer, physician, teacher, preacher, artist and man of affairs? It is impossible, and yet the people are often so unreasonable as to look for just this encyclopædic ability in their minister. The "wholesome practical training" that the Christian minister needs has grown in recent times to as great an extent as solid learning. The same necessity for an elective course, and the prolongation of years of study arises in the practical part of our work as in the scientific. It is evident that it is no longer possible for any one man to fulfil all the requirements for a Christian minister. The time is rapidly passing when congregations will be content with the services of one man. The splitting up of the people into little denominational congregations, which has gone to such extremes in modern Protestantism in this country, has brought the Church into the gravest perils because of the inability of the ministry to do the work required of them. As they vainly strive to do everything, they often fail to succeed in anything.

There must be a consolidation on such a grand scale as to be nothing else than revolutionary. The small congregations must be consolidated into great ones, and the denominational congregations must unite into comprehensive Christian churches served by a presbytery of ministers. This is the ancient way, and that of Christianity in the greater part of its history, and so it is demanded again by the economic forces of our age as well as by the necessity for a complete Christian service. Then there will be one minister as the executive man of affairs, versed in ecclesiastical law, another in pastoral affairs, another a skilful teacher, still another a soul-stirring preacher, others active Christian workers—a well-organized and equipped body of Christian ministers.

This may be difficult in villages where a single minister may be all that it is possible to support, but in these there are not the same extensive demands for variety of work as in cities; and the smaller congregations may be associated with others in neighboring villages, and so several ministers may be helpful to each other in their various gifts.

A "wholesome practical training" presupposes certain aptitudes given to a man by birth or in regeneration. Experience shows that several different aptitudes do not, except in rare instances, exist in any one man. The man himself does not ordinarily become conscious of his gifts until a certain amount of education and training has brought them out. Therefore a general training should precede specialization, as for the physician and the lawyer.

If the one purpose of the Theological Seminary were to train preachers of the Gospel, we might concentrate the wholesome practical training upon that. The prophetic office is regarded as the chief function of the Christian minister in Protestant churches, emphasized because of its neglect before the Reformation.

St. Paul tells us that it "pleased God by the foolishness of preaching to save them that believe" and that "the preaching of Christ is the power of God and the Wisdom of God." We cannot exaggerate the importance of training the intending minister in the preaching of the everlasting gospel of Christ.

At the same time it is evident that many of the most pious and gifted men can never become real preachers. A preacher is born with certain natural gifts and graces which cannot be given by any education or training whatever. Many of the best students do not succeed in the ministry because they have not the gift of preaching demanded by the people; and there is no sufficient provision in most congregations, as at present organized, for the employment of the gifts with which these ministers are endowed. The exclusive emphasis laid upon this part of the work of the ministry and the neglect of other parts is rapidly emptying our churches of intelligent people; because there are few ministers capable of holding their attention by their sermons.

Everyone knows the difficulty of procuring preachers of a high order for important positions. It is not that the average is any lower than in former times, but that there is a much higher standard to which fewer can attain. The reasonable way to overcome this difficulty is to have fewer preachers and better ones. Let the fewer preachers address larger congregations into which the smaller ones should be consolidated, and let the main body of the ministry devote themselves to other forms of ministerial work just as important for the growth of the Church as preaching. Those that have the gift of preaching should receive a richer and larger practical training. This our noble Director, the late Morris K. Jesup, saw when he endowed a Graduate Chair for the higher training of preachers in this Seminary, in order that students so gifted might spend several additional years both in theoretical and disciplinary training for the prophetic work of the Christian ministry.

The Christian prophet has two functions—that of teaching and that of preaching. Some men excel in one of these gifts, some in the other. Few can be successful in both. The original Presbyterian and Congregational Churches in Great Britain and America had often two ministers, the one a teacher, the other a preacher. The preacher and teacher have quite different gifts, training and aims. The teacher aims to instruct the mind of his auditors that they may observe and think. The preacher aims at the will and the emotions, in order to arouse the people and stimulate them to action. The preacher is trained to use all the resources of rhetoric and oratory to accomplish his purpose. The teacher uses the principles of the science of education. The teacher must be more thoroughly trained as a specialist in the subject he has to teach. The preacher needs a more general training, especially in choice literature and the fine arts. The department of Christian pedagogy has ordinarily been neglected in the Theological Seminaries, but I am happy to say that the most recent addition to our Faculty in the Skinner and McAlpin Chair amply provides for "wholesome practical training" in this department also.

There are ample opportunities in this city for training in the practical work of Sunday Schools, Bible Classes, City Missions, Young People's Associations, benevolent enterprises of various kinds, Charity Organizations and Settlement Work. Through the munificence of the widow of one of our most honored Directors, we have an ample endowment for the oversight of this kind of work, and the students are ready enough to undertake training in these interesting fields.

It is in the more strictly professional activities of the minister as physician of souls and church governor that there is the least "wholesome practical training" in our Theological Seminaries. This is not due to any fault in the teaching of Pastoral Theology, which, from the foundation of the Seminary until the present day, has been in the hands of veteran pastors of our leading city churches, but to circumstances which we have not yet been able to control. The rise and growth of Christian Science, Faith Cure and other, the like "practical radicalisms" are the revenges of human nature against the neglect of pastoral medicine by the Christian ministry. They can only be overcome by the recognition of all that is good in them, and by the wholesome practical training of intending ministers in the work of the Christian priest.

The work of the minister as a Church governor has always been considered theoretically in lectures on Church government, but no adequate provision yet exists for a thorough practical training in the law, discipline and government of the Church. I can from long experience in ecclesiastical courts testify to the evil results of so great ignorance of the practice of the law and discipline of the Church. It is folly to have canons of law and books of Discipline when the government of the Church is put in the hands of men who have little if any knowledge of them.

A theoretical knowledge of the work of the minister as pastor and Church governor is as insufficient as theoretical knowledge is to the physician and the lawyer. It is difficult, however, to give this kind of practical training to the intending minister in the Seminary, for we naturally shrink from merely trial exercises, or any kind of unreality, in our service of God. Furthermore, the Churches forbid the most important of these exercises to any but those whom they have licensed or ordained. We have been trying for some years to make arrangements for the service of our students as assistant ministers after graduation, in order that they may thus have their practical training in the real work of the Church, while they continue their scholarly study in the Graduate Department. This is the ideal for which we are striving. But it is evident that funds are required for the support of such assistant ministers either by endowments in connection with the Seminary or appropriations by the Churches themselves. The Churches are improving in this respect, in some denominations more than others; and we may hope that in time we may thus overcome our remaining defects and give the theological student a *complete* " wholesome practical training " for the Christian ministry.

The success of the kingdom of God in this world depends in great measure upon the practical efficiency of the Christian ministry. If one considers how far short the education and training of the average minister falls from the ideal, and how incomplete even the best-trained man is, in view of the immensity of the work of the ministry as a whole, it is surprising that the Church is so successful as it is. We recognize with the apostle that " we have the treasure of the divine grace in earthen vessels that the excellence of the power may be of God and not of us." We know that God will fill these vessels to their utmost capacity with this treasure if only we will use them in giving it to our fellowmen. " For we are laborers together with God."

There is no labor so difficult and yet so inspiring as to work for the eternal salvation of our fellowmen. Nothing can be so awful, and yet so joyful, as to labor together with God. To take part with the Supreme Being in the accomplishment of this divine purpose is the greatest of honors, and in itself the supreme reward.

Conclusion

The ideal of the study of Theology comprehends the three constituents, " vital piety," " sound learning," and " wholesome practical training "; it involves that these shall be intertwined in just and harmonious proportions, and that all the great variety in these departments shall be summed up in a higher unity. This is the work of Theological Encyclopædia, which does not indeed attempt to give a summary statement of the *contents* of all types of religion, all theological learning and all Church work; but does strive to do the *formal* work of organizing them all into a complete and harmonious system, in which each department will receive its just place and importance, without detriment to itself or intrusion upon others. It also sets forth the varied and distinctive methods for the study of Theology, and the helps, literary and otherwise, necessary to do the work.

This Seminary has had an introductory course in Encyclopædia for nearly forty years, entitled by its first teacher, Dr. Philip Schaff, *Propædeutic* or Introduction to the Study of Theology; but it was not until the Graduate Department was established, by the appointment of the present encumbent to the first Chair in the Graduate Faculty, that the higher work of Theological Encyclopædia was undertaken, of summing up the whole work of Theology into a higher unity.

And just here it is important to speak of the Library of the Seminary, which is, or ought to be, Theological Encyclopædia embodied in Literature. We have a Library which is one of the richest in the world in some departments of Theology, and one of the poorest in others. The poverty is due to the fact that the funds at the disposal of the Directors for the Library have always been so meagre. The richness is owing to the purchase, by the Founders, of the Van Ess Library, the most valuable theological library that has ever crossed the ocean; and to the special gifts of many honored givers, the chief of whom are the late Director, David H. McAlpin, and his children, continued for the past forty years. Nothing is more needed than funds to supply the deficiencies of the Library and make it adequate for the use of the Faculty and students in the harmonious proportions that the ideal of Theological Study requires, and to make it more fully what it has always been, the theological section of the Public Libraries of the city.

There was attached to the Chair of Encyclopædia, Symbolics or Comparative Theology, which rises above all the differences of religious denominations into that higher unity in which they agree, and endeavors to consider their differences in religion, doctrine and institution from an irenic point of view. That is especially necessary for this Seminary, which claims to be something better than undenominational or interdenominational: namely, as the late statesman bishop, Henry Codman Potter, delighted in saying "*supradenominational.*"

What Comparative Theology stands for as regards the Christian religion, Comparative Religion represents for all the other religions of the world. We must recognize that the great mass of mankind, now as well as for the millenniums of the history of our race, have been religious in the exercise of other types of piety, in thinking other kinds of doctrine, and employing other practical measures than those familiar to us in the Christian religion.

The Theological Seminary cannot safely ignore these other Religions. They must be studied with a sympathetic spirit, glad to recognize all that is good and valid in them, and with the same irenic purpose that is necessary to reconcile the differences existing in the Christian Church. We cannot any longer take the position, born of ignorance, that God has limited the bestowal of His grace to those who are Christians. We cannot limit the influence of the divine Spirit to Christian lands. We see in Jesus Christ our Saviour "the true Light, which coming into the world, lighteth every man" (John i: 9). We are assured with St. Peter that "in every nation he that feareth God and worketh righteousness is accepted with him" (Acts x: 35).

How can Christianity be the *universal* religion unless it recognizes, with St. Clement, that the Philosophy of the Greeks was as truly a preparation for Christianity as the Law of the Hebrews: and that the practice of ancient Israel of taking up into the Old Covenant Religion elements of good, especially from the Babylonian and Persian religions, and of the ancient Church in appropriating from the Greek, Roman and Oriental Religions valuable material, is the true and wise course for modern Christianity to adopt, by enlarging this theory and practice so as to comprehend all of the Religions of the world. They are all in their way preparatory for Christianity, and will, as we anticipate, eventually be absorbed into a higher, broader and more perfect Christianity, that will be world-wide in its conception, and which will think nothing alien to it that is proper for union and communion with God.

The Graduate Department is not limited to the comprehensive studies thus far mentioned, but embraces advanced work in all departments, Biblical and Historical, Doctrines of Faith and morals, theoretical and practical, where the Professors are at work, busy as bees, searching the foundations, and all that has thus far been acquired, by the exact methods of sound philosophy and scientific criticism, to extract the honey of wisdom, conserving all that is real, true and valid, and eliminating it from all that cannot endure the tests of truth and righteousness, reaching out in all directions to win everything that is right and good for the service of God. I have mentioned the more comprehensive studies because they have their special place and importance for the Graduate School of Theology.

It is just this expansion of Theology into such a great number of studies, overlapping and entwined with so many other departments of human learning, that makes it impracticable any longer to conduct the study of Theology apart from the Universities. The Theological Seminary and the University are in mutual need of each other. When this became evident a few years ago, relations of courtesy and mutual help were established between this Seminary and Columbia University, largely owing to the wisdom of our Director, the Honorable Seth Low. This was subsequently extended to the New York University and to other institutions also. While these relations are valuable to undergraduates they are still more valuable to graduates. For it is just in the higher and more comprehensive ranges of Theology that relations with the University become necessary. It is indeed an important part of the work of Theological Encyclopædia to consider the relation of all education to Theology, in the most comprehensive classification of all knowledge, professions and arts.

The sad warfare that has too often been waged between the partisans of Theology and Science has no place in the higher ranges of Theology. It could never have taken place except upon its lower levels. The ideal of Christian Theology is to recognize all that is good and useful in all human knowledge, in all human activities and in all life, and to build all into a temple of divine Wisdom.

Theology is now, as ever she must be, divine knowledge. She is by nature, as the daughter of God, gentle, patient, loving, and most gracious, welcoming all learning and all workers of good to the feast prepared in her hospitable palace. But she has been too often misrepresented by evil spirits, who have for a season usurped her place.

An ancient Hebrew sage saw a counterfeit of Wisdom seated upon a lofty seat at the door of her house, ignorant and clamorous, with loud, imperative voice, urging the passer-by to turn in and drink of her stolen waters and eat of her secret, soul-destroying bread. Divine Wisdom herself is busy in her palace providing a feast for her guests. She sends forth her maidens with the invitation:

"Come, eat of my bread and drink of the wine I have mingled.
Forsake Folly and live; and go in the way of understanding."
(Prov. ix:5).

And so St. Paul conceives of the household of God, the embodiment of Christian theology, as:

"Built upon the foundation of apostles and prophets, Christ Jesus Himself being the chief corner-stone; in whom each several building, fitly framed together, groweth into an holy temple in the Lord; in whom ye also are builded together for a habitation of God in the Spirit." (Eph. ii: 20–22.)

Our Founders may have had this passage in mind in their ideal, for it is a Theology at once vital, constructive and efficient—*vital* in union and communion with God in the Spirit—

constructive, building on Jesus Christ as chief, and on apostolic foundations, and on all teachers and workers in all ages; their several buildings all fitly framed together in comprehensive unity—and *practically efficient:* growing ever higher and larger into that completeness and perfection of structure worthy of the God of Glory and of Grace.

VIII

THE RESPONSES AT THE DINNER

THE RESPONSES AT THE DINNER

Mr. Robert C. Ogden:

Ladies and Gentlemen, Faculty, Alumni, and Students of the Union Theological Seminary:

I have to say to you all on behalf of the Board of Directors at this close of a remarkable day in the history of the Union Theological Seminary that we as a Board feel under very great obligation to you that you have accepted our invitation for this evening's enjoyment.

The day has been a remarkable one. Its peculiar features have been celebrated in public address at the new buildings of the Seminary to-day, and it would ill become me to undertake any repetition of what has been so ably said already.

At the outset of this proceeding this evening I think it would be well to drink to the toast, "The President of the United States," and before calling for that toast I desire to state a word or two about the present incumbent of that high office. Last Spring we called upon him to give him an invitation to be here to-night. He was extremely gratified and said he would be delighted to come, for he had certain things in his mind on the subject of Religious Education that he would very much like to say and he would like to say them on such a propitious occasion as this, but that he could not tell then whether he would be able to attend when the time came. From the nature of that conversation I was prepared for a disappointment, and the conspiracy between the Panama Canal and the Congress of the United States so worked upon him that he could not follow the bent of his own inclination and be with us to-night.

He has sent us a word of greeting, however. His secretary writes on his behalf:

"The President wishes me to express his regret at his inability to accept. He is working at great pressure on his annual message and it would simply be impossible for him to leave Washington at this time."

I think that as this is a sort of Christian Temperance

Union we may fill our glasses with pure water, and drink not only to the office of the President of the United States but to the President.

After the drinking of the toast, in which all present joined with great enthusiasm, MR. OGDEN continued:

The Union Theological Seminary has been honored in the proceedings of this day by the large number who are representatives of other institutions, who have accepted the invitation to be present. One hundred and thirty-five delegates from other institutions of learning from every part of America, and some not from America have been here with us today. Included in these acceptances we have responses from Oxford, and from Cambridge, and from the University of Durham, and from the University of Manchester, in England; we have them from the University of Marburg, in Germany, together with a number of sympathetic and interesting letters and many acceptances from distinguished scholars in Germany and elsewhere, other than those I have referred to. We therefore feel justified in claiming for the Union Theological Seminary not only a national character but an international reputation, and we are certainly gratified at the sympathy expressed through our sister seminaries, and in such a marked degree by the great universities of Europe.

We shall hear from two of the representatives of those universities, one of them the honored President of Columbia, the other the Bishop of Massachusetts, as the evening proceeds.

And this reminds me that I have here some little remark to make concerning the extent of the program of post-prandial prattling that we have proposed this evening. We have quite a number of speakers, and some people evidently are a little anxious under the circumstances as to the time as to which this dinner would adjourn. I beg of you all to accept my assurances that all of the addresses this evening will be of the most interesting character; and if you will examine the list of the speakers you will be assured I am right. But they are all impressed, being sensitive and honorable gentlemen, with the prominent thought in New York society to-day, which is the thought that is given to us by the Pennsylvania Railroad with the elegance and completeness of its terminal facilities. And this applies to human corporations quite as well as railroad corporations; and I am sure that this beneficent and soul-satisfying thought is prominent in the minds of all the gentlemen that will speak to us this evening.

The first toast on the program, as you may possibly have noticed, is the one entitled " Our Neighbors."

Being a somewhat serious and perhaps partially well-educated group of people, in the words of the Holy Scriptures, we may remember the question of one of the great teachers years ago, " Who is my neighbor?"—and when the Union Theological Seminary asks that question the response comes very quickly, " Columbia University," and therefore it is proper that we should first hear this evening from the loved and honored President of that institution, Dr. Nicholas Murray Butler.

President Butler:

Mr. Ogden, Ladies and Gentlemen:

It is my privilege to state in a few brief sentences my conception of the significance of the coming of this Seminary to its new home on Morningside Heights. It is significant for this metropolitan city and for the Union.

No matter how devoted we may be to peace, we fall inevitably into the habit of speaking of many of the problems and tasks of life in terms of struggle, of contest and of controversy. The biologist and the economist alike will have it so.

We are engaged in a most conspicuous fashion in this modern democracy of ours in making a struggle almost desperate in character for the formation and expression of the intellectual and the spiritual life.

The first act of a good general is to mobilize his forces, to bring them into touch, into relation, into sympathetic co-operation, each part with the other, that the struggle may be more effectively carried on.

It is now almost a quarter of a century since the far-seeing men of New York have begun to occupy and fortify Morningside Heights as the citadel of our intellectual and our spiritual life. They have planted there a great cathedral with its spires of aspiration pointing everlastingly towards Heaven. They have built there a great hospital with its rooms open to receive the poor, the sick and the needy. They have built there a great university representing every aspect of letters and of science in their theory and in their applications.

And now they have surrounded these and their allied institutions with a great school, magnificent, well equipped, catholic and scientific for the study of the " Queen of the Sciences."

One more step has been taken in mobilizing the forces of civilization to fight the everlasting fight and to exalt the no less everlasting ideal.

I remember many years ago to have been present at the service in celebration of the Greek Church's Easter Festival in the City of Jerusalem. I remember that when at twelve o'clock the supposedly holy fire made its appearance at the very center of the shrine there were ready runners stripped and prepared each with his candle, guarding carefully its top with its sacred, divine flame, to carry far away to the churches and the altars and the homes, not alone of Palestine, but to many parts of the distant world where the Greek Church ruled. As these men dashed away from the Church of the Holy Sepulchre carrying this little bit of flame, not one but a hundred poor peasants came up close to put each his little candle where it could get something of this light and take it away to his own hearthstone and domestic shrine. We are building an altar with the everlasting fire. There will be hundreds and thousands and tens of thousands of messengers, and runners and pilgrims to carry out this beneficent light, this guiding purpose, into the uttermost part of these United States and of the world.

We are neighbors in this splendid and inspiring task, and no neighbor, no ally, no friend could be more welcome than the splendid company of scholars who have come under the ægis of the Union Theological Seminary, bearing the great traditions that we heard so splendidly described by Dr. Briggs this afternoon, and taking their part in what is after all the one thing in this life most worth living for, their part in the pursuit of truth and the exaltation of the spiritual ideal.

Mr. Ogden:

Dr. Butler's remarks remind me that I was a little too economical of your time, and still further that I do not propose to occupy but a moment of it now.

I apologize in failing to refer to the location and the completeness of the plant, that so far as we can now judge, is perfect for the accommodation of Union Theological Seminary on Morningside Heights. Those of you who have not seen the buildings, I would advise to see them, and I am sure that if you will carefully preserve and refer to the souvenirs that have been distributed here this evening, and to the views presented there in the latter part of that souvenir, they will, I am sure, awaken your interest. But you should see the buildings for yourself.

The next toast on our program is " The City."

Our honored guest and associate in religious work, the Bishop of New York, is down to respond to that toast, but he has confidentially communicated to me that he does not care to respond to that toast.

I am almost sure that he has forgotten a splendid speech that I heard him make a short time ago on the spirituality of the City of New York, a very wonderful speech, but however that may be, the subject that interests Bishop Greer is " The Union Theological Seminary and its Relation to Church Unity," and on that subject he prefers to speak to us.

THE RIGHT REV. DAVID H. GREER:

Mr. Chairman, Ladies and Gentlemen:

This is a formidable duty to which you have summoned me. Not because of the subject—I can easily get away from that as a preacher does from his text—but because of you, and I cannot get away from you: you distinguished people eminent in so many different vocations, college presidents, teachers, preachers, doctors, journalists, men of affairs, and yet over it all there seems to be a Presbyterian hue, and somehow strange as it may seem, I feel much at home, because I know you so well and I love you so much.

I feel honored with the invitation to your banquet and the privilege which it gives me of extending my sincere and cordial congratulations to you upon the formal and official opening of your splendid seminary buildings. Certainly they occupy a great coign of vantage, not only because of their physical site but because of their academic vicinage. Your proximity to Columbia University will give free and convenient opportunity to the students of the Seminary to avail themselves of the privileges of that great and growing university, over which our learned and brilliant friend, Dr. Butler, so admirably presides.

May I venture to suggest, lest some of you may not know it, that there is another neighbor there on that great eminence —the Cathedral of the Episcopal Church, now approaching one stage of its completion, and perhaps your proximity to that cathedral may have the tendency to divert some of the students of Union Seminary into the ministry of the Episcopal Church. And when that cathedral shall be opened for regular and steady services, as it soon will be, some of your students may be so impressed with the character of its services that they will want to come to us, and if that is the case I am confident of two things: First, that as far as we are concerned they are welcome to come, and, second, as far as you are concerned, from what I have heard this afternoon, they are welcome to go if they want to go. We have no desire to devour them nor they to be devoured; certainly not in the way of which I recently heard when one evening last Summer I was called to the telephone by that imperative ring, and was told by the party at the other end of the wire that the cannibals had just eaten two missionaries, and wanted to know what I was going to do about it. There didn't seem anything then that I could do—it had been done. I can only say that if any of your bright and promising young men desire to come to us, we will try and take better care of them.

But Mr. Chairman and gentlemen, another coign of vantage you occupy. If I interpret aright Union Seminary, it is a great theological university and not simply another theological school. Your faculty, men of international reputation for scholarly equipment and attainment, have it for their aim, if I correctly interpret it, to train for the church at large, the church universal, the church catholic, of any and every name, a learned and competent ministry.

In many ways you have shown this breadth of purpose. I heard this afternoon of the number of representatives, I forget how many, from various denominations you have upon your Faculty and among your undergraduate body. One of your Faculty is a member, a clergyman of the Episcopal Church, and I think he is not exactly what we call among us a "Low Churchman," with ultra-Protestant tendencies; he is nevertheless your honored senior professor. You are not warped, you are not biased, you are not prejudiced, you are not like the Congregational Minister of whom I heard preaching to an assembly, all Congregationalists, in England, take for his text, " If any man refuses to hear the Church, *let* him."

And then, still another coign of vantage you occupy: Your students are from everywhere, not of any particular type or school of thought or temperamental preference, and coming thus together into personal touch and contact, they are perhaps preparing the way by a better mutual understanding for that great union of Christendom and of all Christian forces, which is the desired consummation of the Christian world.

I remember two years ago, when I was present at the

Lambeth Conference in England, and appointed to be a member of the Committee on Reunion and Intercommunion, we were honored once with the presence of the great Congregational Divine, known on both sides of the water, the Reverend Doctor Horton. He told us very frankly and fraternally that the great objection to the Anglican Church, which had been in part responsible for the creation of the Congregational Church, was not the Episcopate, but because the Anglican Church was supposed to be lacking in vital piety and personal religion. And just across the table from him sat the dear old Bishop of Lincoln, now gone to his rest and reward, one of the holiest, humblest and devoutest men in all the kingdom. There they had been, those two great eminent Christian divines, living side by side almost, not quite understanding one another, working and living at cross purposes until they met across the table of a committee room.

If I had time, but I haven't, I would like to speak of that great movement which has recently been started, both in the Episcopal and the Congregational churches, for a conference with the whole Christian world concerning faith and order; not faith as an intellectual proposition, as a theological dogma, as an ecclesiastical tenet, but faith as a stupendous spiritual act, and when the whole Christian world can be lifted up to that first and can live in that first, then and only then shall we be prepared to consider such questions of order as then remain to be considered.

May you in your way, gentlemen, and we in ours, and others in theirs contribute each as each can to that great and desirable consummation.

Mr. Ogden:

When I was a little more active in the Presbyterian Church than I have been of late, I often longed for a real good bishop of the Episcopal sort, and as years lengthen, and as I know the Bishop of New York a longer time, I am sure that the desire on my part does not abate.

I desire to apologize to Dr. Alexander that I slipped over his name as the second speaker on the program this evening, but it was just a lapsus of some sort, and I leave it to the professors of Latin present to finish the sentence, and I now have the pleasure of introducing Dr. George Alexander, who is the nearest to a Presbyterian Bishop of any churchman of our persuasion that I know.

THE REVEREND GEORGE ALEXANDER:

Mr. President, Friends of Union Theological Seminary, Ladies and Gentlemen:

I appeal to you for sympathy. I thought I had obtained my discharge, and it is only a reprieve. I confess to a certain mild surprise that I have been asked to open my lips in this august assembly. The breach between Union Theological Seminary and myself has been steadily widening for a quarter of a century. When I came to New York, one of the attractions was that within a stone's throw of University Place Church stood Union Theological Seminary with Dr. Shedd and Dr. Shaff and others of their confrères. But my type of orthodoxy proved so repellant that within a year Union Seminary sheered off to a distance of three miles, and that has since been increased to six miles, and I assure you, Mr. Ogden, that it is very delightful to receive such a tribute in my declining years, and to have once more the sense of neighborliness and brotherliness.

It is one of the penalties of longevity that one is compelled to note the transition of material grandeurs and the instability of human hopes. I have seen Ichabod written upon the walls of the first home of Union Seminary, and the second home of Union Seminary, which I heard dedicated with prophecies that it would endure through the centuries, has already met with the fate so well described in that bit of Psalmody to which Dr. McKeever and I were inured in our callow days.

Dr. Ogden has referred to me as a Presbyterian. But I suppose it is due to the fact that I am a Presbyterian that I am permitted to sit in this company and respond to this toast. Perhaps I should regard my invitation to speak here to-night as indicating a lingering fondness on the part of Union Seminary for the ancestral home from which she departed nearly a generation ago.

Union Seminary rejoices in her academic freedom and rejoices in her emancipation from ecclesiastical formulas, rejoices in her privilege to enter into affiliations widely embracing other communions and reaching out into other lands, but after all, the most tender and intimate relation of human life is that which binds together mother and child. Union Seminary, after all, sprang from the bosom of the Presbyterian Church. It will be a sad day for both if the mother wholly disowns her child or the child ceases to revere her mother.

Our good Bishop has made a bid for the students of Union

Seminary, and we are willing that he should take all that belong to him, but speaking for the Presbyterian Church we need a lot of them if they are of the right sort. The field is the world, and no small section of the world is this city of ours for which the good Bishop declined to speak.

Let me put in a plea for the Presbyterian Church in the City of New York. Do we realize, gentlemen, that the posts most commanding and most exacting are the posts that are vacant and most difficult to fill. The call is for men; men qualified to meet the demands of the new era in this land and all around the land. That is what Union Seminary is undertaking to do. It is a great and noble task to plant what our President Taft called " Nuclei of Civilization " in every land beneath the skies. For this and for the manning of the churches in our own land we need pastors and teachers, men great in scholarship, if we may have that without the sacrifice of things more vital, but preachers and teachers and pastors; men of God, men of religion; above all, great believers; men with a vision of God and a vision of the world's need that stirs their inmost being.

The Seminary, Dr. Brown, that can do that, that can supply that need will be held close to the throbbing heart of the Holy Church throughout all the world.

MR. OGDEN:

Harvard University is represented in the gatherings of today by a professor who has tender personal ties with Union Seminary, in addition to the honored position that he holds in the great university of Massachusetts, the Rev. Professor Edward C. Moore, who will speak to you on " The University."

THE REVEREND PROFESSOR EDWARD C. MOORE:

Mr. President, Ladies and Gentlemen, Friends of the Union Seminary:

One name has been associated with almost every greater step of progress in the world of education in our country for the last forty years. It is that of President Eliot. Mr. Eliot uttered, a few years ago, a word which I think might well apply to the situation in which Union Seminary finds itself to-day. He said: " He who has been a pioneer in any movement for human welfare has two pleasures. He has the exhilaration of being a pioneer, of blazing the trail. And then, if God grant him but a few good years, he has another joy. It is that of seeing men jostle one another to tread broad the path which he once walked alone."

Such happiness Union Seminary, with a few others which I could name among our theological institutions, may claim. It is the joy of having had its share in the early stages of a movement concerning which one hardly needs to be a prophet to declare that it has made plain the road, which the institutions of sacred learning in this land will be bound to follow.

It is the movement for the association of the training of men for the ministry with the training of men for other professions. It is the path which is to lead to the organic relation of divinity schools to universities and the representation of sacred learning in those centers in which all other branches of learning are fostered.

It may be interesting, however, to remind ourselves that in this association of theological education with the life of a university, for which Union Seminary in its new location stands, we are but resuming a great tradition of the past. We do but revert to a principle which formerly obtained. Indeed, that principle has been interrupted in its application for but a comparatively short period in the history of our own country and in the practice of the Christian Church.

The preparation of men for the ministry was a part of the business of all our older colleges, the ones which have more recently grown to be the most conspicuous of our universities. I pass almost daily through a gate on whose wall is chiseled an inscription, the last few lines of which read thus: "After we had provided necessaries for our livelihood, reared convenient places for God's worship and settled the civil government, one of the next things we longed for and looked after was to advance learning and perpetuate it to posterity, dreading to have an illiterate ministry to the churches when our present ministers shall lie in the dust." Those phrases express the purpose of the founding of Harvard College. From its very inception that college, which has become our oldest and foremost university, set itself this task. It was to prepare men for the Gospel ministry in company with men who were preparing for other walks in life. It was to maintain sacred learning. With allowance due for the peculiar circumstances we might say of the origin of our most ancient institutions of learning the same thing, which is true of the rise of the great schools of the Middle Age in Europe, that the universities had their beginnings in the theological schools.

The first chair in Harvard College, which had an endowment directly attached to it, was the Hollis Professorship of Divinity, founded in 1721. The third such chair in Harvard College was the Hancock Professorship of Hebrew and Oriental Languages, founded in 1764. Their incumbents were college professors. There was indeed no university, in the sense in which we now use that word, in the land. But still less was there a Theological Seminary in the land. The college was the seat of all learning, with sacred learning in the midst. At a much later period of its history when the university would gladly have divested itself of the responsibility of administering those funds, the Supreme Court refused it permission so to do, and informed it that it must continue to afford instruction in those subjects.

Then came the second period in the relation of sacred learning and ministerial preparation to the universities. It is the period of the theological seminaries. It is the period of an impulse with which indeed we have been familiar. And because we have been familiar with it we have perhaps assumed that it belonged to the normal state of things. I refer to the impulse which led to the founding of schools for the preparation exclusively of ministers. These schools have been, for the most part, under strict denominational control. They have been bound often in the most stringent fashion to the maintenance of denominational statements of faith. They have in some cases purposely dissociated from other institutions of learning. Or again, even when they have existed in the same town with those institutions, they have had no more to do with them than had the Jews with the Samaritans. I say that, through familiarity, we have assumed that this was the normal state of things. In simple truth it is but a brief episode in the history of learning in our country. And furthermore, it is a state of things with difficulty made intelligible to the inhabitants of other countries.

The first of these isolated institutions, Andover, founded in 1807, did indeed represent a vigorous and conscientious revolt against the liberal movement which had possessed itself of Harvard College. But in some measure also it represented the fear of the influence of the rationalist movement which was felt in all our colleges. It did not then look beyond a fixed curriculum of professional studies, for which a few chairs sufficed. It stood for an ideal of the contemplative, not to say other-worldly and ascetic life of the minister, for which meditation and seclusion formed a valuable part of preparation. The lead of Andover was followed within two decades by almost every greater community in the United States. There passed over the whole country a wave of denominationalism of which the founding of many of these institutions was an expression. They did noble work. They raised up a ministry not merely faithful but able. They made a contribution to the life of our churches and country and to the evangelization of the world which can never be forgotten.

And yet practically every one of the principles which I above alluded to as lying at their foundation is to-day in dispute. Under the challenge of the world, through the pressure of its needs with our own enlarging and historical and social sense, we have come to feel that the man of God must be thoroughly furnished with all good work, not merely for that of the institution which calls itself the church. We feel that the church is itself no isolated institution let down into the world. But it is a great factor of the world, bone of its bone and part of its very life. We feel that the so-called sacred learning is no small and separated province of the world of learning, but it is a vital and integral part of that same. We feel that the institution of theological learning can never do all that its students need if it stands by itself. We feel that a course of study has but scant right to be called such if the results of its investigations are all known and fixed beforehand. We feel that the walls of denominationalism, which these institutions have done so much to build up, ought now to come down. We feel that these institutions, in which men of one church are gathered to the exclusion of all others, run some risk of hindering the union of Christ's Church on earth. We feel that a school, in which youth of many churches are united in work and prayer, is more likely to further that union. Under these convictions, which are more and more widely shared, we are treading the course which will lead us, not backwards—thank God, we do not go backward—but will lead us forward into an association of sacred learning with the life of the universities far broader and more magnificent than that which in former years obtained.

The Harvard Divinity School also, despite its background in the seventeenth and eighteenth centuries of which I spoke, passed through this same experience of segregation. It is true that the men who drew up the articles constituting that school in 1817 used these remarkable words: "No assent to the peculiarities of any denomination of Christians shall be required either of the instructors or students." They were thus the precursors by nearly ninety years of those who, in 1905, proclaimed Union Seminary free from any act of subscription and opened its doors to professors and students of many churches. Yet for sixty years those remarkable words described a theory rather than a fact. Indeed it would hardly be too much to say that even the theory was sometimes lost sight of. The Harvard Divinity School was in fact as simply a denominational school as were the others. And it had hardly more to do with the university, whose name it bore and under whose authorities it was governed, than had some of the isolated schools to which we have referred. It was in fact, if not in charter, a Unitarian School. It did a noble work for the Unitarian Church. But in the mood which ruled the age it would do little or nothing beyond that area. Without doubt many of its constituency had no desire to do anything beyond that area.

Then came the third period when, thirty years ago, the university declared that it would not hold itself responsible for the maintenance of a denominational school. It set before itself the ideal of a true university school, in which the two implications of its charter were really carried out. It set before itself the ideal of a school in which men were chosen to teach because of a learning and character which made them the acknowledged compeers of the teachers of any other subject. But in their choosing no other consideration was to have any weight whatsoever. It set before itself the ideal of a school in which students of theology, if they wished to study philosophy or history or science, had all the treasures of the university to draw upon. It set before itself the ideal of a school in which, if a student under any faculty whatsoever wished to give himself to one or more of the studies relating to religion, he had masters in those subjects for his teachers. He was not compelled to do this work in a sentimental and amateurish way in strong contrast with the seriousness of all the other work he did. If he wanted to learn something, for example about the New Testament, why should he not be taught by somebody who knew something about the New Testament? It sets before itself the ideal of a theological school, in which the spirit of a university obtained, in which the same courses were accepted for several degrees, in which students mingled upon equal terms, in which the wholeness and sacredness of life was emphasized and sustained exactly by the recognition of the society and nominality and human loveliness of religion. Truly a great ideal. But is not this the ideal to which Union Seminary hopes to render unexampled service by all the unrivaled equipment in which we rejoice as she enters upon her new era with this day?

The representative of the most famous of the isolated seminaries said to me only a few years ago: " But think how much it will cost us to move." I could only reply: " But did you ever think how much it will cost you not to move? You will have to multiply your faculty by five to give to the men what they rightfully demand. And if you do not give it to them, they will go elsewhere." They did go elsewhere. That institution has since moved. And now men are seeking it again. I believe that the contention was right. I believe that the movement is irresistible. For not even if the isolated seminary should multiply its resource by five could it do the work so well as by passing over that work to the university to be done by standing shoulder to shoulder with the university. It is a matter of atmosphere. It is a spirit and life. Men are to be educated for the ministry not merely as other men are educated, but they are to be educated with other men, as part of the world of educated men. They are to look into the eyes of other educated men with understanding, and not across a great gulf fixed. They are not merely to live and work for other men, but they are to live and work with them. The dual standard of life and interpretation of the Gospel, which was the curse of the Middle Age, still lingers. It is the secret of the alienation of many from the church and the ministry. It must be done away.

Oh, and let me make an even greater appeal than that and one not so often made. It is not merely that the theological student needs the university. It is also that the university needs the student of religion—so only that the latter be a person of the genuine quality which anybody can need. I have spoken of the contribution which the university makes to him. But is there nothing which he can contribute to the life of all the other members of the university? Truly nothing and less than nothing, if his religion is of the artificial sort. Truly nothing, if he bring reproach upon his cause. But he has an inestimable boon to confer if he be the right sort of a man, a pure youth among the tempted, unconquerable idealist among many who are sordid, generous among many who are selfish, Christianlike among those who have found Christ, and, as well, among those who have not, a minister by life, example, saintliness of spirit, even before he came to the ministry in the word of the Gospel upon which his heart is set. I have charge of a university chapel. I have no more faithful supporters in my work than the Divinity School men. It would indeed be disgraceful if it were not so. But the university is indefinitely richer by the fact that it is so. Or, from this matter of character to recur for a moment to that other matter of learning of which I spoke. Why should the other members of a university be deprived of the study of religious subjects altogether or else condemned to study them in an unlearned and an unscientific way? Why should not the circulation of the free life of learning be just as good for one set of men as it is for the other? I stand here to plead for this side of the question, and that most ardently. It is a great opportunity which the old endowed universities have in this regard. For, apparently, it is a problem which the universities under state control find much more difficult to solve. I know a school of which it would be true to say, that hardly a man has taken his degree there for twenty years who has not taken one or more courses in every year of his residence from a professor who was not a member of the theological faculty. But the parallel fact seems to be even more interesting. In that same interval there have been few years when there have not been from three to five hundred men from other departments of the university taking instruction under members of the theological faculty. You understand, these were men who were not going into the ministry. They were men who were going into the law, or medicine, or business. One result of all this has been that the old barrier, which used to be thought to separate theological education from any other, has been done away. I can remember a time when I myself thought of a theological professor as a man of altogether different sort from any other, a theological student as a being of an inferior sort, his studies far less rigorous and his standards far more exacting than other standards. Now one standard obtains for all. Fees are equalized. The mendicancy of the profession is done away. The standing of theological learning in the world of youth, who after all are soon to be the laymen in our churches, is redeemed in a manner which, for the future of the church, as it seems to me, is important in the highest degree.

We speak often in our times of the naturalization of Christianity within the life of the different races to whom the Gospel has been preached. We mean with that phrase to describe that contribution which the various peoples have made and are now making to the interpretation of Christianity. We mean that modification of the understanding and application of Christianity which has taken place through the assimilation of it to the life of different nations. One of the subjects at this morning's session in connection with this dedication was that of the adaptation of the Gospel in the work of missions. The Gospel is one thing to the children of Arabia, it is another to the Hindoos or the Chinese or the Japanese. The Gospel lives for all of these peoples in terms of their own culture.

But that which we thus conceive as to differences of race and place must be true also as to differences of time. There is a constant need of the adaptation of the Gospel in the spirit of a new time, a naturalization of it within the culture of each succeeding age. The Gospel was one thing in the first century, it was quite a different thing in the third. It was one thing in the seventeenth century. It must be quite a different thing in the twentieth. The Puritan did his work in the world because he was profoundly convinced that his statement of religion was true. But not only that. He easily convinced his hearers that that statement was true. He did that because the statement really was germain to the whole intellectual life of the time. It was an integral, a vital, a congruous element of the culture of the age. The trouble with us in our time is that too often we seek to bring religion to men in a statement and interpretation which is incongruous with the cultivation of the age. It may be dear and familiar to us. But it is alien to many men. It has no power over them. It speaks a language which they do not know. It needs naturalization within the vivid and vigorous life of our own time. We shall then first stand firmly upon our feet and speak the Gospel again with courage and with power, when we speak it in words that men understand and in its vital relation to all the other things which they understand. Then and then only will men feel Christianity to be a part of life, and all life to be interpreted and crowned in religion. There is no problem whose solution is more vital to the church. And for the solution of this task Seminary and University will need to work, not in hostility the one to the other, nor even independently the one of the other. Together, working hand in hand, they are to be the instrumentalities for the accomplishment of this aim, which is so much to be desired.

Mr. Ogden:

Our next speaker, as announced on the program, is the Reverend Professor Henry Van Dyke, whom we honor alike for his literary abilities and for his capacity as a great preacher, but he is sick and not able to be here.

He writes an interesting note to Dr. Brown, the closing words of which are these: " I could only croak with a voice like a raven, but croaking will be out of place at the banquet, so I will be present in the spirit and wish health, a long life and vital powers to Union Seminary with all my heart. Faithfully yours, Henry Van Dyke."

We have no one to fill his place.

I have been very much comforted from my lapse of memory a little while ago apropos of Dr. Alexander, by remembering that Dr. Butler was to-day the delegate appointed by the Manchester University in England, but it slipped off his memory and into his " forgettery," and he left his gorgeous raiment hanging in its closet and came simply in the ordinary academic garb of the President of Columbia University. That had a nearer relation to the whole proceeding to-day because we have with us an honored friend. We should love to welcome him as the Right Reverend William Lawrence, we should love to welcome him as the Bishop of Massachusetts, but he is not himself to-day at all. He is the representative on this occasion of the University of Durham, the most ancient university in England, and so in our academic procession to-day he had the glory of the splendid red gown, the glory that would have been divided with the President of Columbia if the President of Columbia's memory had been a little better.

So I have the pleasure of presenting to you, Bishop Lawrence, who will speak to you about " Our Friends Across the Sea."

THE RIGHT REVEREND WILLIAM LAWRENCE:

Mr. Chairman:

For two or three minutes I am going to speak for myself. I am not from across the sea. I am from the Colony of Massachusetts Bay, where Calvinism in all its points is honored, and where, with the rising of the sun each morning we arise still and say the Westminster Creed. I came here not from across the sea but as a friend, and I came, not because I was invited, but because I wanted to.

As Dean of a college or the Theological School rather that thirty years ago in its infancy tried to plant itself close to the greatest university in the country, a university then supposed to be under the cloud of Unitarianism, I come to tell you that from our experience to be in the neighborhood of a university is good.

Now I come to my more formal words. Through the chance that I hold an office for a while I have been honored by two universities, that of Durhám and that of Cambridge, and I may say honestly that I figured for Durham in a Cambridge gown to-day. But it was all honest, because Durham knew it, and they told me to. By chance, I say, of holding that office and through no merits of my own I have been honored by those two universities, and therefore may speak for a moment for those two, or perhaps for one or two other English universities.

My first words, therefore, as representative of an English university are in the form of a question. We in old England remember Presbyterianism of three or more centuries ago, and some of us suffered under it; and now here we are and we see these exercises, and we witness this dinner, and we note the presence of the representative of Harvard University, and of the President of Kings College of New York, and of the Bishop of New York, and other representatives of the Anglican Church, and we ask the question, is this Presbyterianism when it has come to its full fruition?

My next remark is one of wonderment. Do we of the ancient Universities of England hear that in this school there are five representatives of different denominations, and among the students studying theology to-day are representatives of twenty denominations? Do we understand that? Are we dreaming? Is it possible that in the new country the churches have come to that, and the Christians have come to that, and that young men and old men can study theology together in the spirit of the love of truth, and in the fullness of charity, and that without yielding to one or another their faith or holdings? If that be so, God be praised, for our traditions in England are such that we have been unable to do that; but God be praised that a land has risen where that can be done.

And a word of congratulation and of God-speed. Now we begin to see how America has worked out the problem of Christian thought and love and of spiritual freedom. You by the separation of Church and State, with all your laws, avoid questions of which you still don't know the nature. With freedom of Church, liberty of thought, with the readiness on the part of the Church to let every man seek his own way in the seeking of the truth, we have such confidence in Christ, the truth, that we believe that in that freedom there will be a grasp of Christian truth and a search for Christian love and a consummation of Christian character that is beyond that that has been the fruitage of any Christian nation up to this day.

Therefore, in the name of old England we give you of the new country in all your Christian aspirations and in your spirit of full liberty, we give you God-speed.

MR. OGDEN:

Those two last speeches were from Boston.

There sits down here just in front of this table a modest, quiet man from Boston who furnished us all the final designs and has superintended the construction of the buildings whose dedication we celebrated this afternoon.[1]

There sits at this table a member of the Faculty of the Union Seminary who as a business man can give points to a great many people who are engaged in worldly professions, a man who has been of the greatest possible service to the building committee as he has been to the architects, and whose reputation as a scholar is one of the glories of the Union Theological Seminary.

I refer to the Reverend Professor George William Knox, who will have a few words to say to us about the Seminary.

THE REVEREND PROFESSOR GEORGE WILLIAM KNOX:

Mr. President, Ladies and Gentlemen:

It is my privilege to respond for the Faculty of the Seminary and to express our pleasure, brethren of the Universities and of the Churches, at your presence with us to-night and also in the occasion of this assemblage—the completion of the group of buildings on Morningside Heights.

For years we dreamed our dreams and saw our visions, and often the doubt arose that these were too good to be true. Yet, as ever in the providence of God, it has proved that our highest visions and dearest dreams were not good enough to be true, for the realization surpasses our most ambitious anticipations.

Deeper than the joy which fills our hearts is our sense of indebtedness and of obligation. First of all to the noble laymen who through so many years have stood strong in support of ministerial training, making this Seminary possible in the

[1] The reference is to Mr. Francis Allen, the architect who designed the seminary buildings.

beginning, throughout its history enlarging its facilities, adding to its resources and now crowning all by the splendid gift which we celebrate to-night. We remember them with deep gratitude, sensible of the responsibility the guardianship of their gifts involves.

We would next acknowledge indebtedness to the Board of Directors for their attitude toward us. In our day we hear much of a certain aloofness of Directors from Faculties, but in this instance there has been thoroughgoing co-operation. It was characteristic of the policy adopted by the Board from the beginning that when Mr. James, its Vice President, made his great gift, the Faculty were asked to prepare a statement of needs. Months were given to the study, and when the plans were completed they were embodied in the program prepared for the architectural competition, without addition, subtraction or modification. As I have indicated, the instance is typical, and the Faculty is never unmindful of the friendship, the confidence and the co-operation given fully and freely by the Board.

We would acknowledge also our indebtedness to the architects, to Mr. Allen and to Mr. Collens, who gave our plans the artistic realization which excites the admiration of all who view the new buildings. Their skill, their familiarity with the traditions of Gothic architecture, their clear conception of what was desired, made possible the realization of our dreams. Never in all this work have they permitted their keen artistic sense to interfere with utility; never did men work in closer sympathy with their clients or strive more earnestly, even in the smallest details, to meet their wishes. So long as these buildings endure will the sons of Union Theological Seminary recognize their debt.

Not only do we feel our indebtedness to givers, to Directors and architects, but we recognize our indebtedness to the Universities of New York. Our long friendship has not been distant nor casual, but intimate, and the debt has been ours. There have been the heartiest co-operation and the freest liberty. Our students have been welcomed to the class-rooms and we have welcomed the instruction that they have there received. Our harmony with the University is not some chance reconcilement of theology with science, for there is no trace of that supposed antagonism, and this is not because we compromise or ask compromise, but because we recognize that the instruction of the University in many subjects like biology, psychology, sociology, history, philosophy, is given as we would have it given, without fear and without favor by men intent upon knowing and teaching the truth. We do not look upon the university as something foreign in which we have no part, for in earnest seeking after truth there is no distinction between scientists and theologians—for where truth is there is God. Moreover, the so-called hostility has passed because to-day the method of theological study is none other than the method of the sciences. We may have our differences, as biologists differ from psychologists, but beneath all such superficial diversities is the deep unity that comes from a spirit devoted to truth and from the understanding that in the same way and by the same methods all truth is to be attained. Thus recognizing our indebtedness, it is our desire that it may be repaid, though only in part can it be repaid.

We recognize our indebtedness to men without representative here to-day, who were not present in the Chapel this afternoon and yet without whom our dreams would have remained dreams, without whom all the artistic skill of the architects would have been futile. We recognize our indebtedness to the community of so-called common men, to the men who dug the stone from the foundations, who laid it strong and well, to the artisans of every class, the representatives of more than fifty trades, to the laboring men of New York. From an intimate association with them in the two years past, I bear testimony to their faithfulness, their thoroughness, their ability, their earnestness, their honesty, their thoroughgoing sympathy with their work. While we dwell in the structure which they have reared, which, alas, has known the death of some of them, we shall hold them in grateful remembrance and recognize our debt.

Recognizing this indebtedness to benefactors, Directors, architects, universities, artisans—a question presses for an answer—what return can Union Seminary make, what gifts has it for the community which has made the Seminary possible? What gift has religion for this age, this democratic, scientific, progressive age whose watchword is evolution, whose philosophy is the philosophy of change—for this age with its marvelous advance in things material, with its sublime self-confidence and throbbing life? What gift has religion for this city, for its financiers, its students, its artists, its politicians, its artisans, its endless varieties of sorts and conditions of men? Can Union Seminary help to answer that question?

These buildings constitute for us a challenge. In some way this great question will be answered so that the state and nation and lands beyond the sea shall understand that as in the ages past religion wrought its message into the life of the race, so for our time also it has a message, true, essential, vital. That we may have our part in forming this answer will be our repayment of our indebtedness—that it shall be answered we know, as we believe in the God of truth whose we are and whom we serve.

Mr. Ogden:

We are fortunate in having present as one of the representative guests on this occasion the Reverend President James G. K. McClure, of McCormick Seminary in Chicago, who will speak to us on "Our Sister Seminaries."

The Reverend President James G. K. McClure:

Mr. Ogden, Ladies and Gentlemen:

The message that I am to bring you to-night is this, in two words, Congratulation and Confidence. The Seminaries that are represented here to-night, widely scattered as they are, diversified in their form and teaching, are interested most deeply in that which has been spread before our eyes to-day. Every casual observer has been immediately impressed by the beauty and the accommodations of the buildings, but we who represent the Seminaries have examined these buildings from the lowest basement to the topmost story, and we have noted how complete in every respect is the provision for the work that is to be done. We congratulate Union Theological Seminary not alone upon the material plant which is the most stately and dignified of all institutions of the kind in the world, but we congratulate Union Seminary upon this assemblage of to-night.

We know the experiences of our own lives, when we were facing the great question as to whether we should give ourselves to the ministry or not, and we recall our prayers which brought us into sweet fellowship with God.

We know that gathered here to-night are men, ministers and laymen who have come to express the high hope that every wish that Union Theological Seminary has for herself may be fully accomplished, and that there shall be indeed beautiful piety here, and profound scholarship and application to all the needs of humanity. That is our word of congratulation, and it is from a full heart.

Our other word is a word of confidence, confidence in the product of the Theological Seminary, the ministry. We believe with our whole being that there is no need so great in the entire earth as the need of the minister of God who goes to spread the ideals that are so essential to the truest welfare of the people, and who professes the faith so that the vision of God becomes clear, and who sees it in its relationship to society and to true righteousness before God. The man who can lift the heart of his brother up to highest heaven is the man of all the earth in his kingship and in the dignity that God has conferred upon him.

The glory of the ministry is a wondrous glory. Here tonight we sit in our luxurious surroundings. The graduates of this Seminary are scattered to every portion of the earth, many of them in little bits of places where they are dealing with hardships that are scarcely intelligible to us. Those men in their places, doing the work that God has assigned to them, are our brothers: this Seminary has given them, and they are for the glory of God and the good of the world.

What I long for when I see such buildings as these is that not only out of the homes of the common people, out of the homes where thrift is a necessity, there shall be brought the young men who are to be our ministers, but that out of the homes of the greatest wealth there shall come the consecrated sons who shall have refinement bred into them from all the atmosphere of their home surroundings, and who shall be able to go anywhere and everywhere and stand in perfect equality with those of the highest gifts and station; who shall always have back of them, as they preach the truth as God has revealed it to them, such a substance of material power that they are elevated above mere dependence upon salary, and can sway men as a man sways his fellowmen when they are upon the same platform of equality.

And this, also, is what I wish, that we who believe in God—and once again register our belief—when we have given scholarship and when we have given the appeals of piety, and when we have set before men the appeals of truth, that we insist that every man of them shall have a character of personal piety. Blessed is the man that shall always create an atmosphere wherever he goes, making it evident that he is a man of God, so that the wicked man shall be rebuked in that presence, and the discouraged man find the vision of heaven open to him with a new benediction.

And I have a second word of confidence. The Church of

Jesus Christ—I do not attempt to make a definition of it, though to me it consists of those who believe in the God and Father of our Lord Jesus Christ, and rejoice in worship, fellowship, and the advance of the Kingdom—the Church of Jesus Christ to-day in her potentialities is sufficient for the needs of the hour. We hear so often criticism upon our weakness, upon our inability to cope with that which to-day is calling for solution. In spite of this the Church is being led on step by step; but she will be led by very rapid steps in a very short time, for Christ is in his Church, and he is with us all and these problems are to be solved: and the ministers that Union Theological Seminary is preparing, and all other Seminaries are preparing, through the Church are to bring in the Kingdom, and it is to be a glorious Kingdom, sufficient for the needs of every man, the highest as well as the lowest.

Before I go away to-night, I have another word of confidence, confidence in the purpose of God. There is such a purpose. The good pleasure of God is that to such as ourselves, instructed in this and other seminaries, and those who were under us, shall be given the Kingdom.

Some years ago, when the Westminster Confession was being revised, the Committee which had in charge the work visited Washington, and audience was given them at the White House, and Mr. McKinley courteously turned to one of the Committee and he said, "I hope that in the revision you will not take out 'predestination.'" The representative of another communion, a brother of Charles Wesley, said, "Who can resist His will?" And I believe that there is no man anywhere in our world who understands what the ministry is striving for, what the mission of the Church is, what the needs of mankind are, what the problems of the present are, who does not realize strength in the fact that he can look up into the skies and he can believe that there is an Eternal Purpose. He himself has seen its effect. All through history there comes the direct assurance in fact that evil cannot live, that good must live, and that there is the instruction for every minister, "Fight against Cæsar." And as we separate to-night I would have every man of us go out with the voice of triumph on his lips. Union Seminary and all our Seminaries are set to do a mighty work, the remaking of the human heart, the bringing of the manhood into the likeness of Jesus Christ Himself, and that is the result that we seek, and you and I, representing the Seminaries that are near to our hearts, must part to-night knowing that the purpose of God will not fail.

Mr. Ogden:

It is all summed up in the title of the next speech, which will be on the "Spirit of Service." The speaker will be the Rev. President William H. P. Faunce, of Brown University.

The Rev. President William H. P. Faunce:

I seem to be the only barrier left between this assembly and one whom it is eager to hear, President Brown. I promise you that this barrier will very speedily vanish, but not until I have offered greeting to this Seminary from the city of Roger Williams.

In the old meeting-house where we hold our annual commencements, at the foot of College Hill, there is a quaint inscription on the old church records of 1775, which reads: "This meeting-house was built for the worship of God, and to hold commencements in." That shows how education and religion were united in the minds and the hearts of some of our founders of the institutions of our eastern states.

Every building is a confession of faith. Somehow a man's creed gets itself uttered in the structure he erects. Oftentimes the building expresses the faith more deeply than any possible formula. I would not judge a whole nation by a single instance, but is there no suggestion in the fact that the central building of London and Great Britain is the House of Parliament? In that nation where freedom "has slowly broadened down from precedent to precedent," there the home of law, and of liberty under law, finds the central place. And when we cross the Channel—again I would not generalize from a single instance—is there no suggestion in the fact that the center of Parisian life is the opera house?

What faith, then, is here confessed in the superb new structures of Union Theological Seminary? Certainly a profound faith in religious education; in religion as central in human life; and in the Christian prophet as exercising indispensable function in a democracy. Clearly also the Seminary has here put in buildings its faith in the closer articulation, the essential unity of the modern church and modern society. This style of architecture is one which no school in this country probably would have attempted fifty years ago. The old-time college or seminary buildings incorporated the Puritan individualism. Each structure on the hill at Andover Seminary stands plain, severe, rectangular, owing no allegiance to any other building on the horizon. The buildings of Newton Theological Seminary, where I studied, have a similar isolation and obliviousness to the presence of any other structure. But here in Union henceforth will be preached each day, in this unified group of buildings, our faith in the solidarity of society and our prayer for the visible unity of American Christianity.

I have attended three great educational functions during this autumn. One was the inauguration of the President of Smith College, where I saw seventeen hundred women students—the largest assemblage of women ever gathered for educational purposes in one institution. The second was the very brilliant function at Bryn Mawr College—whose president is happily with us to-night—when that college celebrated its twenty-fifth anniversary. But this function at Union Seminary we must acknowledge does not suffer in comparison with any academic festival that has gone before.

It will do New York City good to have a " School of the Prophets " loom big in the public eye. It is good for " the city of the flatiron " to be also the site of magnificent structures devoted to the equipment of the modern prophet. It is good for the city of sky-scrapers and railroad stations and subways to have also a great habitation for ministers of the Christian faith—a habitation which no traveler can ignore, of whose existence no business man can long be ignorant.

Without the prophets all our captains of industry and all our scholars will lead us astray, for the function of the prophet is to tell us what is worth while; to give us the true perspective of life in the twentieth century. We have no great background of history as has Europe; no long ancestral customs like the orient. We see things vividly, instantaneously, as it were by snap-shot, and we confuse the things of passing moment with the things that abide. It is good for this city to be told in clear voice what is worth while.

When the beloved former president of this Seminary passed into the unseen, I took up a newspaper and found a dozen lines devoted to his great career, while two columns in the same journal were given to the death of a famous race horse. It is useless to find fault with the newspapers in such a case. It is you and I, it is the city of which we are a part, which is to blame—exalting the thing of the moment and ignoring the essential. The prophet is to make us see the difference.

So I want to tell you that institutions far outside the metropolitan district rejoice with you. Denominations outside your own are getting weary of questions of procedure and ceremony, and long for the essential verities of the Christian faith. Every man who is filled with such longing must be glad to-night in your gladness. At these tables we see the foreglimpse of the time of which William Watson sang—if I may change one word in his musical verse:

> " The coming of the morn divine,
> When churches shall as forests grow;
> Wherein the oak hates not the pine,
> Nor beeches wish the cedars woe;
> But all in their unlikeness blend,
> Confederate to one golden end."

MR. OGDEN:

The last number is " Retrospect and Prospect," to which the head of the Union Theological Seminary, the Rev. President Francis Brown, will respond.

THE REV. PRESIDENT FRANCIS BROWN:

Mr. Ogden and Friends of the Seminary:

We appreciate all the kind words that have been spoken, and the tribute which this assembly has paid to the Seminary. It is too late either to spend time in reviewing the past or to attempt any elaborate sketch of the future, but we are glad to have offered the occasion for a meeting like this, for the notable presences that have graced it and for the significant words that have been uttered in it. And if, as you carry them with you in your minds—these strong, able, clear words—you will associate with them some thought of the Union Theological Seminary, we shall be glad of that too.

It might seem to an onlooker as though the occasion of this day's celebration and of this great gathering were a very small one—two hundred students, twenty instructors—what is that compared with the thousands of the great institutions? The real significance of it all has been expressed here more than once to-night. It simply means that you as well as we are in your inmost hearts aware that the world is ruled by things out of sight, and that the testimony of things out of sight is that testimony which wins a response from the deepest depth of the human heart, and that the reality of the things out of sight is the reality that controls the world.

We are trying—and we know in some measure the difficulty of our task—we are trying to express the old religion in terms that can be understood by the new generation and that can lay hold of the heart and conscience of that generation. It is no light thing to undertake, and we do not claim to be alone in undertaking it, but we feel ourselves committed to it. We try to express in our actions, as in our words, our sense of human brotherhood without losing our religion in our brotherhood, and in all our activity we are conscious that we are only servants and not masters, and we desire to be used and not simply to control.

Most of our work is very quiet, apart from public gaze. We publish some books; few of you read them—and why should you read them? We offer some public lectures, some courses of sermons, occasional indications of our presence in the community; but after all our real, steady work is quite out of sight, and there it must remain, like the work of all teachers, except as its result appears at some remove in time and space from our workshop, and in a connection where few if any can think of the workshop from which it came—and that is all as it should be.

But we shall be glad if, when the temporary impression of this day and this evening is fading out of your minds, you will still sometimes remember that we are all the while, and year after year, trying earnestly and patiently and quietly and with what power we have to accomplish this service, which is a service not to ourselves but to you and to the community of people, reaching on and on throughout the world—and to God to whom the world belongs.

We are not ashamed to say that we still need the aid of those who can aid us in material things. No institution ever had such friends as we have had and have. It is their generosity and the place in which they have set us that enlarge our needs. And I speak of this only that you may not be surprised, or think us grasping, if now and then you learn of some appeal from us for things we need to do a larger work for our Master.

A single last word of retrospect. I remember, and some of those here will remember, how the year after we entered the home of the Seminary on Lenox Hill, Doctor Hitchcock observed the thirtieth anniversary of his connection with the Seminary, and in words of deep feeling, few but choice and powerful, he referred to the history of those past years, and the strong lives that had filled them. Then he told that story of Kossuth, who, when he was here long ago, spoke for Hungary, and in the midst of an impassioned period, suddenly stopped and stood silent for half a minute, and then brushed his hand over his face, and said, "Pardon me, gentlemen, I saw the shades of my ancestors!"

At a time like this we see the spirits of those whose bodies are not here with us, of those who, humanly speaking, ought to be standing where we stand, and sitting where we sit, and we rejoice to know, as in our hearts we do know, that their sympathy is with us and that their souls rejoice.

And now as we look forward, we do it not without some touch of apprehension and yet not without a large and radiant hope. You may not always agree with us: you will, I think, believe that our wishes at least are high, and our purposes not wholly ignoble, and we beg of you to feel that you and we are united, and united with all people throughout the world who aim at the best things, in "looking for and earnestly desiring the coming of the day of God."

www.ingramcontent.com/pod-product-compliance
Lightning Source LLC
LaVergne TN
LVHW010607110826
845149LV00003B/809

* 9 7 8 1 4 1 8 1 8 7 3 5 4 *